OUR PLANET

Infographics for Discovering Planet Earth

Text by

CRISTINA BANFI

Illustrations by

GIULIA DE AMICIS

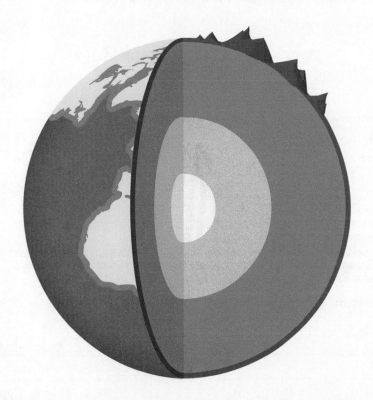

For permission requests, please contact the publisher at:

Mango Publishing Group
2850 Douglas Road, 4th Floor
Coral Gables, FL
33134 USA
info@mango.bz

For special orders, quantity sales, course adoptions and corporate sales, please email the publisher at sales@mango.bz. For trade and wholesale sales, please contact Ingram Publisher Services at customer.service@ingramcontent.com or +1.800.509.4887.

Our Planet

ISBN: (p) 978-1-68481-032-1 (e) 978-1-68481-033-8
BISAC: JNF051180, JUVENILE NONFICTION / Science & Nature / Earth Sciences / Geography

Printed in the USA

© 2021 White Star s.r.l.
Piazzale Luigi Cadorna, 6
20123 Milan, Italy
www.whitestar.it

Translation: TperTradurre s.r.l.
Editing: Michele Suchomel-Casey

1 2 3 4 5 6   25 24 23 22 21

Originally published in Italian by White Star, 2021

Cristina Banfi

Cristina has a degree in Natural Sciences from the University of Milan in Italy. She has been involved in scientific communication and fun learning for over 20 years and has contributed to numerous school textbooks and educational publications, mainly for children and teenagers. In recent years, she has written several books for White Star.

Giulia De Amicis

After receiving her master's degree in Communication Design in 2012, Giulia started working as a visual designer and illustrator. Her work mainly consists of presenting visual information for environmental newspapers, magazines, and associations, with a specific focus on marine ecology, geography, and human rights. In recent years, she has illustrated several books for White Star Kids.

CONTENTS

INTRODUCTION

Earth is a unique and wonderful planet, and it's also the only one where we know life exists. Earth is our home, and that's why it's important to know all its secrets.

This book is jam-packed with amazing information and curious facts, and when you've finished reading it, you'll know how the Earth was made, what's inside it, how mountains are formed, why the ground shakes sometimes, what a stalactite is, and what makes this planet so special...

You might be surprised to learn that Earth's hard, outer shell is actually very thin, kind of like the skin of an apple, whereas deep inside the planet, there's Earth's iron heart, surrounded by hot molten rock that sometimes rises to the surface, causing spectacular eruptions and forming volcanoes.

You'll definitely feel better knowing we're protected by a shield made of air. Not only does it protect us every day from being hit by objects from outer space, it also gives us wind, rain, and sunshine.

And if you're an animal lover, you can explore the habitats they live in, learn about their adaptations and behavior, analyze data, and do size comparisons. Page after page, you'll travel from the depths of the ocean to the highest peaks in the world, from polar ice to dense equatorial rain forests, passing through rivers, forests, deserts, and savannas, learning all about the ecosystems' most interesting characteristics.

If you pay attention, you'll see that our planet is very fragile and in need of protection. Humanity is exploiting Earth's resources, which often destroys environments and endangers plants, animals, and humans alike. Instead, we must respect and protect our home for every creature that will live on our planet in the future.

STRUCTURE OF THE EARTH

Earth is one of an infinite number of planets in the universe. It's part of our solar system, together with seven other planets, and it's the only one with an oxygen-rich atmosphere and bodies of liquid water on its surface. Above all, it's the only planet we know of so far that's inhabited by living things.

It's the third closest planet to the sun and is rocky, just like Mercury, Venus, and Mars, while Jupiter, Saturn, Uranus, and Neptune are composed mostly of gas.

Its radius, or the distance from the surface to the center, is 3,963 miles (6,378 km), making Earth the fifth largest planet in the entire solar system.

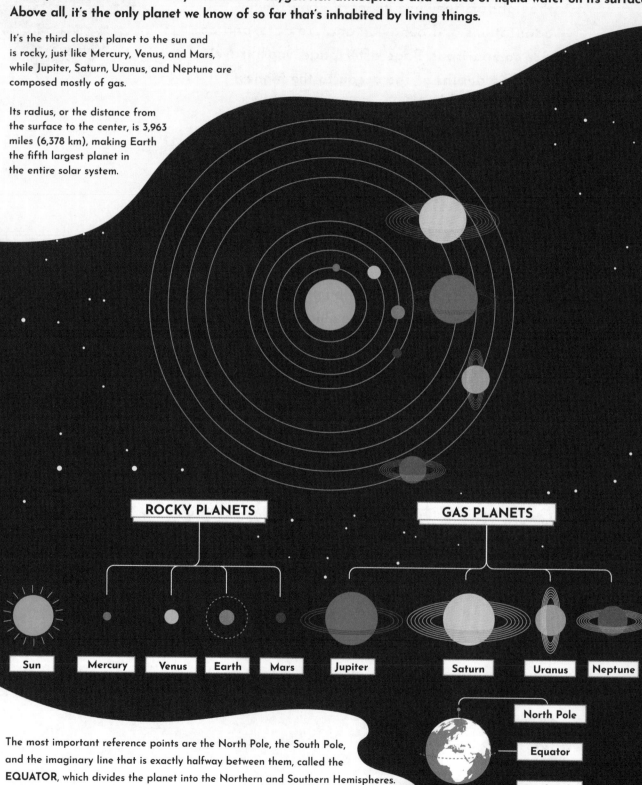

ROCKY PLANETS

GAS PLANETS

| Sun | Mercury | Venus | Earth | Mars | Jupiter | Saturn | Uranus | Neptune |

North Pole

Equator

South Pole

The most important reference points are the North Pole, the South Pole, and the imaginary line that is exactly halfway between them, called the **EQUATOR**, which divides the planet into the Northern and Southern Hemispheres.

Although it looks like a ball, Earth isn't actually perfectly round; it's slightly squashed at its poles and swollen at the equator.

As a result of this bulge, gravity is weaker at the equator, and you will weigh less here than you would if you were standing on one of the poles.

The Earth moves

REVOLUTION

Although right now you are sitting still while reading this book, you are actually moving at 67,000 miles (107,826 km) per hour! This is the speed at which Earth moves through space. It doesn't move randomly, but follows a very specific path around the sun, about 93 million miles (150 million km) away. This path is what is known as Earth's **ORBIT**.

Earth's orbit is not a perfect circle, but rather an ellipse, and the sun is not exactly in the middle. This means that Earth is closest to the sun in early January and farthest from it in July.

Earth's revolution around the sun and its tilted axis of rotation—causing the Northern and Southern Hemispheres to be at different angles to the Sun—are what cause the seasons to change.

It takes Earth 365.2564 days to travel all the way around the sun. Our calendar year is 365 days, so to compensate for the extra quarter of a day, every 4 years, a day is added to the end of February. This is called a leap year.

REVOLUTION

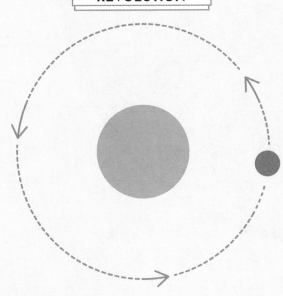

ROTATION

As well as revolving around the sun, Earth also spins on its axis.

This means that everything on Earth's surface also rotates, but at different speeds, depending on where on Earth an object is located. If you were somewhere on the equator, you would be moving at a maximum speed of 1,036 mph (1,667 km/h), whereas if you were standing on the North or South Pole, it would seem as if you weren't moving at all.

The rotation of Earth causes day and night.

ROTATION

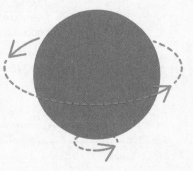

Earth takes almost 24 hours—23 hours and 56 minutes, to be exact—to complete one rotation on its axis.

INSIDE EARTH

Earth's interior is made up of concentric layers, each with its own unique physical and chemical characteristics.

These layers are the **CRUST**, the **MANTLE**, and the **CORE**.

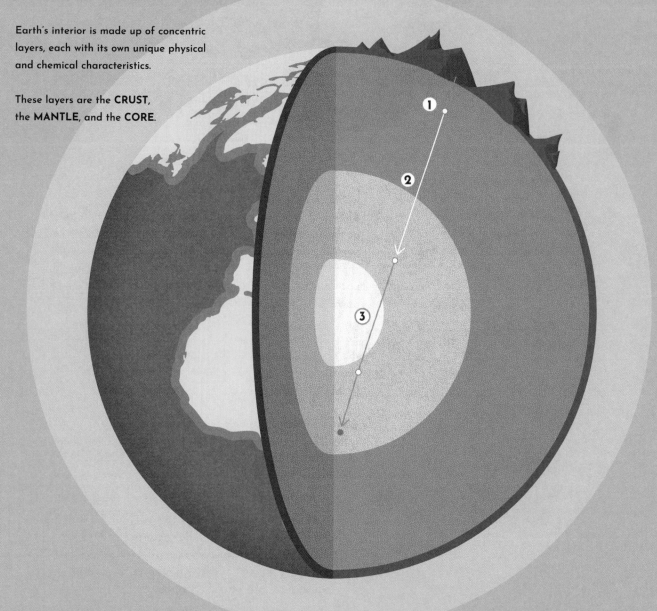

9,032-10,832°F (5,000-6,000°C)	7,232-10,832°F (4,000-6,000°C)	2,552-5,432°F (1,400-3,000°C)	71.6°F (22°C)
solid state	liquid state	mostly solid state	solid state
inner core	**outer core**	**mantle**	**crust**
3,200-3,963 mi (5,150-6,378 km)	1,800-3,200 mi (2,890-5,150 km)	1,700-1,800 mi (2,810-2,890 km)	0-43.5 mi (0-70 km)

1. THE CRUST

This is the layer we live on and the one we know the most about because we can examine it up close. The crust is extremely thin compared to the size of the planet; in some places it is only 5 miles (8 km) thick, while in areas where there are mountains, it can be as thick as 43.5 miles (70 km). Still, this isn't too thick if you think about the earth's huge radius.

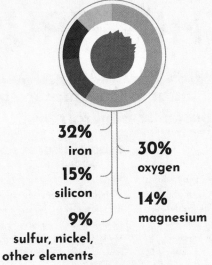

32% iron

30% oxygen

15% silicon

14% magnesium

9% sulfur, nickel, other elements

2. THE MANTLE

The next layer is the mantle, which is about 1,770 miles (2,850 km) thick, making up around 84% of Earth's total volume. All of the elements the mantle is made of are bound together as rocks.

Although the mantle is almost completely solid, it is not rigid and it flows slowly like a liquid. Earth's crust floats on top of it, like a piece of wood on water.

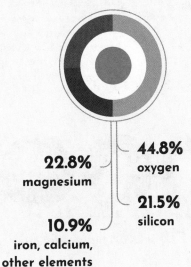

22.8% magnesium

44.8% oxygen

21.5% silicon

10.9% iron, calcium, other elements

3. THE CORE

Earth's core is the "beating heart" of our planet. It has a radius of about 2,175 miles (3,500 km)—just over half the planet's total radius. It is made of two layers: The outer core is liquid, while the inner core, which is as big as the moon and as hot as the sun, is solid due to intense pressure. Earth's core contains a high concentration of two heavy metals—iron and nickel—whose properties are associated with Earth's rotation. They are responsible for the generation of Earth's magnetic field, which protects our planet by deflecting solar wind and the dangerous charged particles it carries.

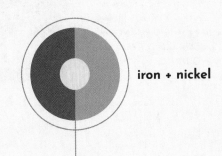

iron + nickel

Earth's core is about the same size as Mars.

A THIN CRUST

Earth's outer layer is solid and rigid. It's made up of rocks, which in turn are composed of minerals.

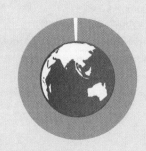

MINERALS

Minerals are substances found in nature. They can be made up of a single element (such as gold, silver, or copper) or of several elements, which is more common. There are over 4,000 minerals on our planet, but only 30 of them are common!

FRIEDRICH MOHS'S SCALE OF HARDNESS

Minerals are very different from each other in terms of color, luster, density, and hardness, or their ability to resist scratching. A German mineralogist named Friedrich Mohs invented a scale of hardness called the Mohs scale. He selected 10 well-known minerals and arranged them in order of increasing hardness, based on how easily they could be scratched.

About **99%** of the minerals in Earth's crust are made up of only eight elements: oxygen, silicon, aluminum, iron, calcium, sodium, potassium, and magnesium.

+ hard

10	9	8
Diamond	Corundum	Topaz

− soft

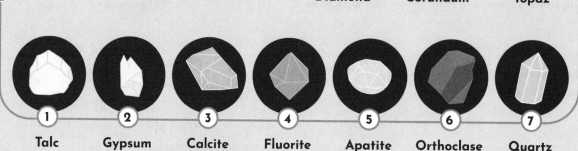

1	2	3	4	5	6	7
Talc	Gypsum	Calcite	Fluorite	Apatite	Orthoclase	Quartz

ROCKS

Rocks don't all form the same way, and therefore they are not all alike. There are three main types of rocks: **IGNEOUS, SEDIMENTARY,** and **METAMORPHIC.**

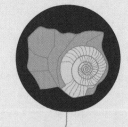

Igneous rocks
These form from the cooling and hardening of magma or lava. When formed from magma inside the earth's crust, they are called intrusive rocks. When formed from lava, they are known as extrusive rocks. Igneous rocks make up 95% of Earth's crust.

Sedimentary rocks
These rocks are the ones most often seen by people. They come from other rocks that have been slowly worn down into smaller pieces by wind, rain, and ice. This process is called erosion. These smaller pieces, called sediments, are then transported by rivers and deposited in layers on the bottom of oceans or lakes. It takes a very long time for the sediments to become compressed into sedimentary rock, even millions of years. Only sedimentary rocks contain fossils.

Metamorphic rocks
These form deep in Earth's crust, where pressure and heat are high. They are usually formed through the transformation of pre-existing rocks. Examples of metamorphic rocks are marble (which is formed from limestone), anthracite, soapstone, and schist.

The brittle crust and outer layer of the upper mantle form the lithosphere, which is divided into huge slabs called **TECTONIC PLATES**. These float on the flowing layer of mantle below, and they move very slowly, driven by the circular motion of the magma.

When the edges of the plates meet, the plates may collide, disintegrate, or slide over each other, producing volcanoes and earthquakes. This makes these areas very unstable.

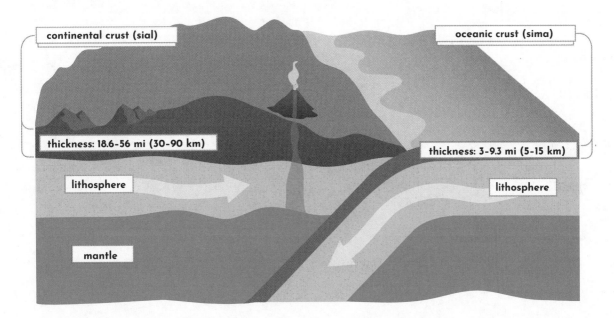

continental crust (sial)

oceanic crust (sima)

thickness: 18.6-56 mi (30-90 km)

thickness: 3-9.3 mi (5-15 km)

lithosphere

lithosphere

mantle

THE SPEED OF TECTONIC PLATES

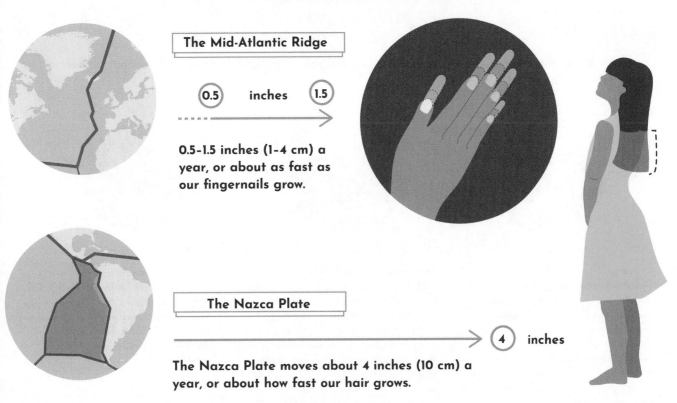

The Mid-Atlantic Ridge

0.5   inches   1.5

0.5-1.5 inches (1-4 cm) a year, or about as fast as our fingernails grow.

The Nazca Plate

4   inches

The Nazca Plate moves about 4 inches (10 cm) a year, or about how fast our hair grows.

There are seven major plates:
African, Antarctic, Eurasian, Indo-Australian, North American, Pacific, and South American.

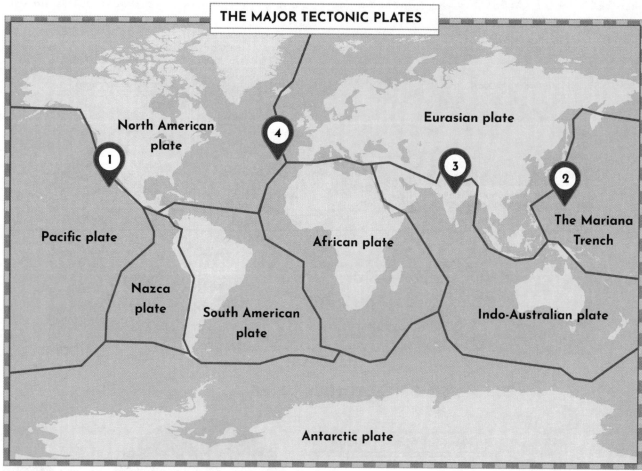

THE MAJOR TECTONIC PLATES

North American plate

Eurasian plate

Pacific plate

Nazca plate

South American plate

African plate

The Mariana Trench

Indo-Australian plate

Antarctic plate

There are three types of plate boundaries:

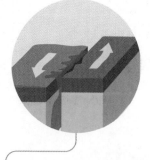

Convergent boundaries: This is where two plates are colliding. If one plate is oceanic and the other is continental, the first, which is lighter, will slide under the second. This process is called **SUBDUCTION**. The oceanic crust is forced into the mantle, where it melts and is destroyed, becoming magma. Part of the magma then rises to the surface and activates volcanoes.

Divergent boundaries: This is where two plates are moving away from each other, causing the plates to split apart. Magma rises from the underlying mantle, and when it cools it creates a new oceanic crust. If the boundaries are on the ocean floor, an underwater mountain range, called a **MID-OCEAN RIDGE**, will form. If, on the other hand, the plates split apart on a continent, a **CONTINENTAL RIFT** will occur.

Transform boundaries: These are found where two plates slide past each other in opposite directions. This friction causes frequent earthquakes. These boundaries are called **FAULTS**. The San Andreas Fault in California is one of the most famous.

1 | San Andreas Fault

Transform boundary between the North American plate and the Pacific plate

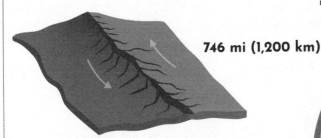

746 mi (1,200 km)

2 | The Mariana Trench

Convergent boundary between the Pacific plate and the Mariana plate

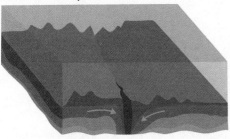

3 | The Himalayas

Convergent boundary between the Indian plate and the Eurasian plate

4 | The Mid-Atlantic Ridge

Divergent boundary that separates the South American plate from the African plate, and the North American plate from the Eurasian plate

The movement of the plates is therefore responsible for the movement of the continents that rest on them. Scientists were able to do a reconstruction showing that about 270 million years ago there was just one supercontinent, which they called **PANGEA** (this name comes from *pangaia*, which means "all the earth" in Greek).

PANGEA
270 million years ago

The movement of the plates subsequently caused Pangea to split apart, first in two and then into several pieces, or continents, which over tens of millions of years slowly moved into the positions they are in today. The continents continue to move, and scientists think that in about 250 million years they will have moved back together again.

15

FIRE CRATERS

When the Earth releases its energy, two often-related phenomena occur: volcanic eruptions and earthquakes.

VOLCANOES

A volcano forms when molten rock from the mantle squeezes out through a crack in the Earth's crust.

This molten rock is called either magma or lava, depending on where it is. If it's under Earth's crust, it's called **MAGMA**. Since it's lighter than the solid rock that surrounds it, magma tends to rise to the surface, surging through fractures and fissures. When magma reaches the surface, it's called **LAVA**.

There are several types of **LAVA**, each with a different chemical composition and temperature range, although all types of lava are incredibly hot.

When a volcano spits out lava, it's called a **VOLCANIC ERUPTION**. But lava is not the only thing to be expelled during an eruption; gases and other materials, called pyroclastic material, are also thrust into the air, often violently—for example different-sized ash, lapilli, and volcanic bombs.

Interestingly, the tiny particles that make up volcanic ash can actually be more dangerous than other pyroclastic material. This is because they can remain in the air for years and can travel to areas that are a long way from the eruption site.

ERUPTIONS

Explosive

1,112-1,832°F
(600-1,000°C)

acid lava

viscous

flows slowly

Effusive

1,832-2,282°F
(1,000-1,250°C)

basic lava

fluid

flows quickly

When the lava is expelled, it then hardens on the volcano, building it higher and higher with each eruption.

Some volcanoes can take thousands of years to form, while others can appear overnight, just like the **PARICUTIN VOLCANO IN MEXICO**, which is considered one of the youngest volcanoes in the world.

Paricutin Volcano

This volcano appeared in a cornfield on the morning of February 20, 1943, and just one year later it was over 1,300 feet (400 m) tall. The eruptions ended on March 4, 1952, after it had reached a height of 10,400 feet (3,170 m) in 9 years.

TYPES OF VOLCANOES

Volcanoes are not all the same.
They can be grouped
into four main types.

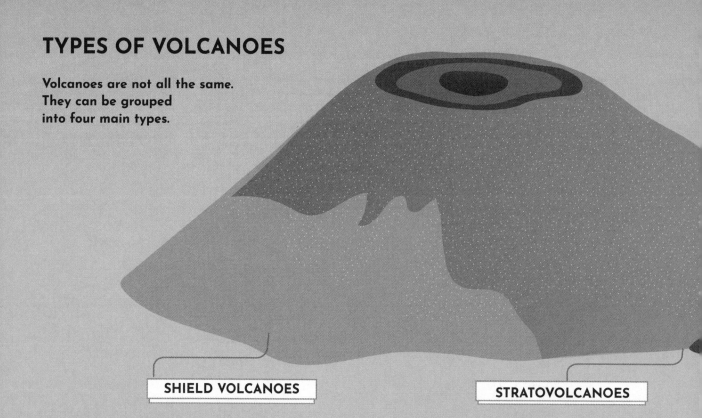

SHIELD VOLCANOES

These volcanoes don't have violent eruptions, and
they produce low-viscosity lava that can flow for
dozens of miles. This means that they are very
wide with gentle slopes. They get their name from
the fact that they look like a shield from above.

Hawaii's **MAUNA KEA**, the tallest volcano in
the world—standing 13,800 feet (4,207 m) tall—
is a shield volcano. It rises from the bottom of
the ocean, so if we measure it from its base, it's
actually 33,474 feet (10,203 m) tall, which is even
taller than Mount Everest.

STRATOVOLCANOES

Stratovolcano eruptions alternate between lava
flows and explosive blasts of pyroclastic material
(ash and rock). These volcanoes have a relatively
narrow base and fairly steep slopes, and they
often reach great heights. Stromboli, off the
western coast of southern Italy, is a stratovolcano.
It is called the "Lighthouse of the Mediterranean"
because it has been erupting almost continuously
for over 2,000 years, producing spectacular,
incandescent explosions.

There are approximately 1,500
potentially active volcanoes
around the world.

About 50-70 volcanoes
erupt every year.

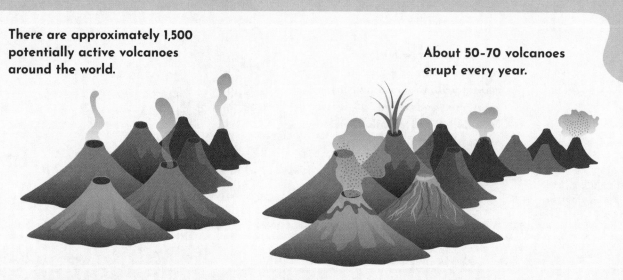

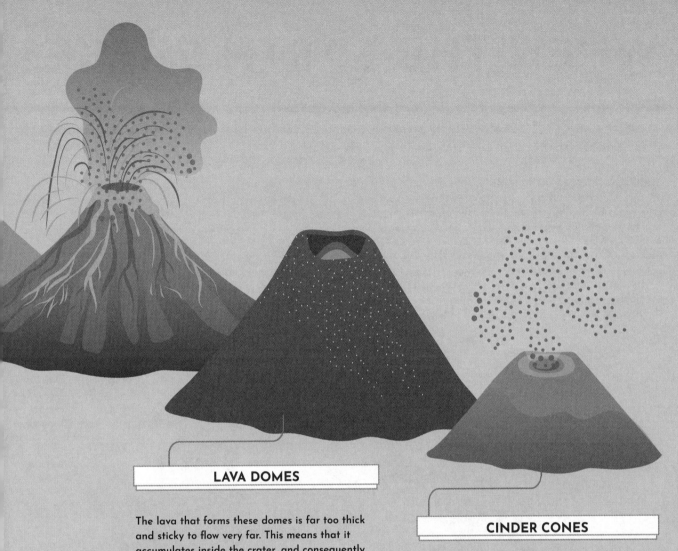

LAVA DOMES

The lava that forms these domes is far too thick and sticky to flow very far. This means that it accumulates inside the crater, and consequently the dome continues to grow. These volcanoes can produce violent explosions.

CINDER CONES

The eruptions of these volcanoes are short-lived, and they generally only expel pyroclastic material. They are smaller than other types of volcanoes, reaching a height of about 1,312 ft (400 m).

At any given time, at least 20 volcanoes are erupting around the world.

WHEN THE EARTH SHAKES

Earthquakes are the sudden, violent shaking of the ground, and they can occur both on land and under the ocean. They usually occur when two blocks of the crust suddenly slip past one another or break away from each other.

WHAT CAUSES AN EARTHQUAKE?

Where the edges of the plates that form Earth's crust meet, the plates are able to slide over each other. But often the plates lock together, and a huge amount of energy accumulates at that point. When this energy is released suddenly, it causes the ground to shake. This is an **EARTHQUAKE**. This energy travels outward from the hypocenter in all directions, in the form of **CONCENTRIC SEISMIC WAVES**, just like those that form on the surface of a pond when we throw a stone into it. The seismic waves travel through Earth, which shakes as they pass.

When the waves reach Earth's surface, they move everything that is on top of it, such as houses and bridges, but also rivers and forests. As they move away from the hypocenter, the waves lose their energy and gradually disappear. There are two types of seismic waves—P-waves and S-waves—and as they travel through the ground, they cause it to shake in different ways. **P-WAVES** cause the ground to move back and forth, like an accordion, while **S-WAVES** cause it to move up and down, like the waves in the ocean.

The P in P-waves stands for "primary." They travel faster and therefore always arrive before S-waves, or "secondary" waves.

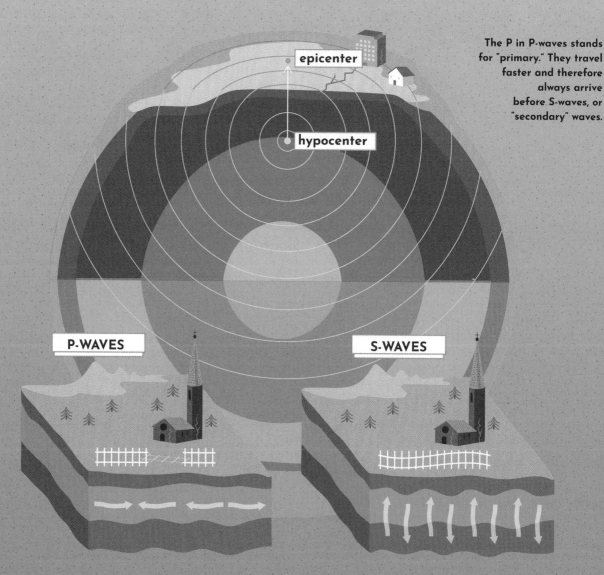

epicenter

hypocenter

P-WAVES

S-WAVES

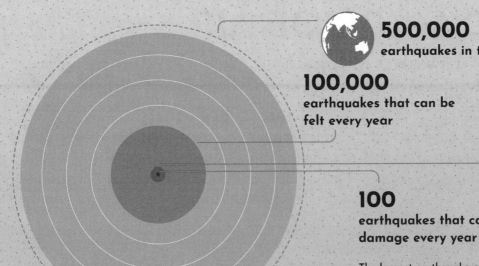

500,000
earthquakes in the world every year

100,000
earthquakes that can be
felt every year

1,500
earthquakes in Japan
every year

100
earthquakes that cause
damage every year

The largest earthquake ever recorded had a magnitude
of 9.5 and occurred in Chile on May 22, 1960.

The deadliest earthquake that we know of was in central
China in 1556. About 830,000 people died.

THE MOST POWERFUL EARTHQUAKES IN HISTORY

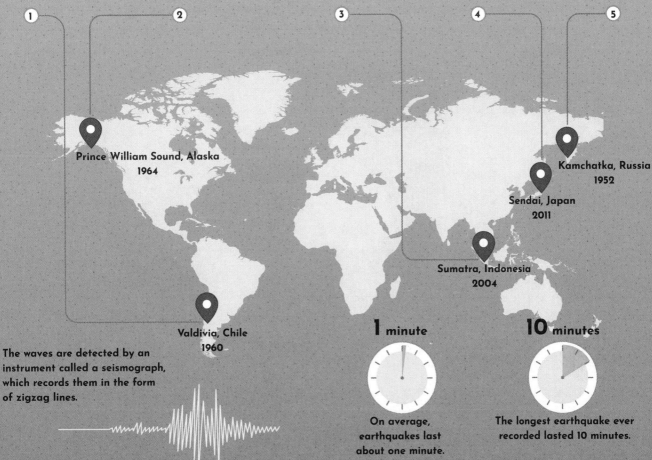

1

2

3

4

5

Prince William Sound, Alaska
1964

Kamchatka, Russia
1952

Sendai, Japan
2011

Sumatra, Indonesia
2004

Valdivia, Chile
1960

The waves are detected by an
instrument called a seismograph,
which records them in the form
of zigzag lines.

1 minute

On average,
earthquakes last
about one minute.

10 minutes

The longest earthquake ever
recorded lasted 10 minutes.

21

A SHIELD MADE OF AIR

Earth is wrapped in a very thin blanket of air,
held in place by gravity. It's called the atmosphere.

78% **21%** **1%**
nitrogen oxygen other

Its density is determined by
how many air molecules gravity
can stop from escaping into
space. The atmosphere is a
mixture of different gases.

① ②

The atmosphere is a shield that protects Earth by absorbing the sun's ultraviolet, or UV, rays, which can be lethal to living things. It also stops rock fragments that float in outer space and sometimes enter Earth's orbit from colliding with our planet. When they hit the atmosphere, they create friction, which in turn creates heat—temperatures can reach 3,002°F (1,650°C)—and this causes small objects to burn up and become meteors. Most of these disintegrate before they hit the ground.

1 Troposphere
2 Stratosphere
3 Mesosphere
4 Thermosphere
5 Exosphere

WHERE DOES THE ATMOSPHERE END?
There is no clear boundary between the atmosphere and outer space because, as you move farther away from Earth, the mixture of gases slowly becomes less dense, eventually fading into space at 932 miles (1,500 km) above the surface. But there is an imaginary line, about 62 miles (100 km) from Earth's surface, that scientists use to define the border between the atmosphere and outer space. It's called the **KÁRMÁN LINE**, and it's used to distinguish where aircraft (below the line) and spacecraft (beyond the line) can fly.

4   5

Kármán line

Seventy-five percent of the atmosphere is within about 7 miles (11 km) of Earth's surface. The atmosphere is not the same everywhere. The composition of the air changes, and the temperature varies with altitude. It can therefore be divided into concentric layers: the lower layers interact with the surface, while the higher layers interact with outer space.

THE LAYERS OF THE ATMOSPHERE

Earth's atmosphere is divided into five layers, and the boundaries that separate them are called PAUSES.

1. TROPOSPHERE

The troposphere contains half of the atmosphere. It extends to about 11-12.5 miles (18-20 km) above sea level. It is the lowest layer and has the greatest influence on our lives. It contains all of the water vapor in the atmosphere, it's where clouds form, and it's where meteorological phenomena take place. The higher you go, the colder the air gets.

2. STRATOSPHERE

The stratosphere starts just above the troposphere and extends to 31 miles (50 km) above the ground. The temperature increases the farther up you go, and there is little water vapor, making the air very dry. The stratosphere is very stable because the air here is thinner than it is at sea level. This is where jet planes and weather balloons fly.

The upper stratosphere has a high concentration of ozone, a molecule that contains three oxygen atoms, forming what is known as the OZONE LAYER. This layer warms the atmosphere because ozone molecules absorb the sun's harmful radiation and generate heat.

In 2013, a skydiver named Felix Baumgartner jumped from a balloon more than 22 miles (36 km) up, in the middle of the stratosphere.

3. MESOSPHERE

The mesosphere extends to 53 miles (85 km) above the surface, but its density varies greatly depending on latitude and the season. The temperature decreases with altitude, and very strong winds make the air unstable.
The top of the mesosphere is the coldest part of the atmosphere, with a temperature of about -220°F (-140°C). This is where most meteors heading for Earth burn up, leaving streaks of light behind them. These are what we call SHOOTING STARS.

4. THERMOSPHERE

The top of this layer can be found anywhere between 311 to 621 miles (500 to 1,000 km) above the ground. The temperature here is influenced by the sun and can be as high as 2,732°F (1,500°C). The air density is very low. This layer is very important for communications because it helps reflect radio waves coming from Earth back to the surface. This is where the International Space Station and most artificial satellites orbit. The thermosphere also contains the ionosphere, which is composed of electrically charged particles. These particles are responsible for the **NORTHERN LIGHTS**.

5. EXOSPHERE

This is the outermost layer of the atmosphere, and very little is known about it. It's extremely thin because it merges into the **ATMOSPHERIC FRINGE**, gradually fading into outer space. It's composed of very widely dispersed particles of hydrogen and helium.

THE COLORS OF THE SKY

The atmosphere is also responsible for the color of the sky, which on clear days is **BLUE**. The color is produced by the effect of scattered sunlight, which occurs thanks to the gases and particles in the air. Sunlight travels in waves, and it's white because it's made of the waves of all the colors of the rainbow. When it enters the atmosphere, it collides with tiny particles that cause the waves of light to split and bounce off in all directions.

Shorter waves, like those of blue light, scatter more easily, so that's why the sky is this color. Longer waves, like those of red and yellow light, travel beyond the air particles and continue on their journey.

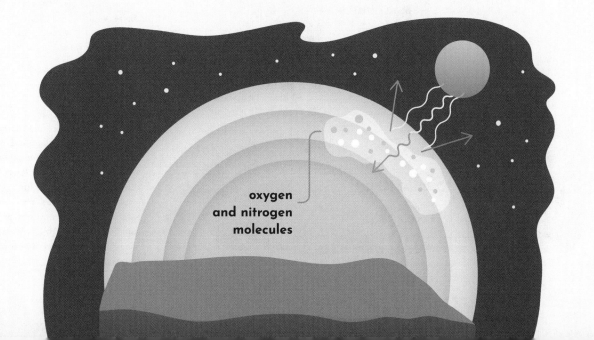

oxygen and nitrogen molecules

ALL ABOUT THE WEATHER

Every day, our life is affected by the weather.
We wait for rain during a drought or for snow so that we can go skiing.
If we are planning an outing, we want it to be a sunny day.

METEOROLOGICAL PHENOMENA are fundamental to life on our planet, and practically all of them occur in the troposphere, the layer of the atmosphere closest to the ground, which is in constant motion. Weather is not to be confused with climate.

METEOROLOGY

The study of weather is based on a combination of:

temperature

humidity

air pressure

WEATHER can be defined as the state of the atmosphere in a specific place, at a specific time. It can also change quickly throughout the day.

The factors taken into consideration when describing weather include precipitation, temperature, wind conditions, and air pressure. When one of these factors changes, the weather changes too.

CLIMATE is the weather of a place averaged over a long period of time (usually 30 years or more).

Climate is determined by observing weather data over many years. The climate can change, too, although much more slowly than weather.

1980   1990   2000   2010   2020

TEMPERATURE
The temperature tells us how hot or cold the air is, and it varies according to latitude, altitude, season, the angle of the sun, and geographic location. The highest temperature ever recorded on Earth was 134.06°F (56.7°C), in July 1913, at Greenland Ranch in Death Valley, California. The coldest temperature ever recorded was -128.2°F (-89°C), in Antarctica in 1983.

134°F (56.7°C)

-128.2°F (-89°C)

HUMIDITY
Humidity is the amount of water vapor in the air. Without it, there would be no clouds, and consequently, no rain. Hot air holds more water vapor than cold air.

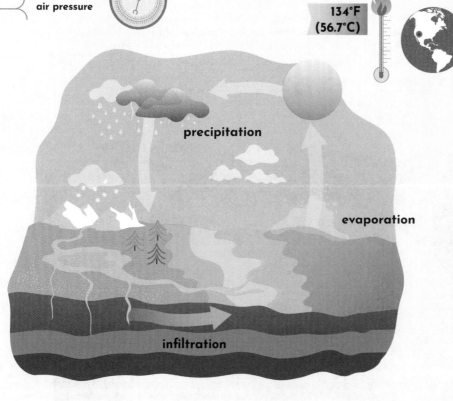

precipitation

evaporation

infiltration

THE WATER CYCLE
Water circulates continuously in the atmosphere. It evaporates from the surface of the ocean and is transpired from leaves in the form of vapor. As the vapor cools and condenses, small water droplets form around microscopic particles of dust called condensation nuclei, thereby forming **CLOUDS**.

CLOUDS

Clouds form in different ways: For example, when a warm, humid air mass collides with a cold air mass or a high mountain, it is pushed upwards and cools down. The water vapor condenses into liquid water droplets, which then form clouds.

Clouds are not all the same, and they don't all produce rain. They have different names based on their shape and their height in the sky. There are three main types: CUMULUS, CIRRUS, and STRATUS.

CUMULUS

These are big, white, fluffy clouds that look like cotton balls. They can develop into altocumulus clouds or cumulonimbus clouds, which produce heavy rain and thunderstorms.

STRATUS

These are flat, low-level clouds that tend to cover much of the sky. They are responsible for all those cloudy days and can produce light rain called drizzle.

CIRRUS

These are wispy, high-level clouds made of ice crystals. They are usually a sign of good weather. They move at high speeds, up to 99 mph (160 km/h).

All other clouds are a combination of these three types.

Cirrus

Cirrocumulus

Cirrostratus

Altocumulus

Cumulonimbus

Altostratus

Nimbostratus

Stratus

Cumulus

Stratocumulus

Fog is a kind of cloud that forms on Earth's surface. It can make it very difficult to see and dangerous to drive a vehicle.

Airplane contrails can be considered clouds: They are formed by the molecules of water vapor that exit the engines, which turn into ice crystals when they come into contact with the freezing air.

PRECIPITATION

Precipitation happens when water falls from the clouds. This water can be in a liquid (RAIN) or solid (SNOW, SLEET, and HAIL) state.

The most rain ever recorded to fall in a week was 16.4 feet (5 m). It fell on Reunion Island in 2007.

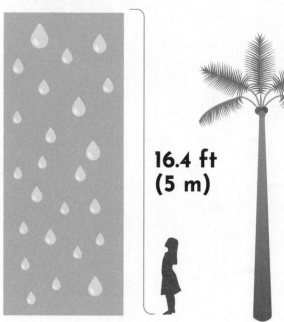

16.4 ft (5 m)

RAIN

Raindrops come in different sizes. Their size and air resistance also determine their shape. Contrary to popular belief, raindrops are not tear-shaped.

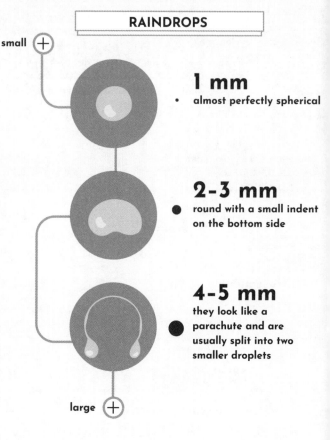

RAINDROPS

small +

1 mm
- almost perfectly spherical

2-3 mm
round with a small indent on the bottom side

4-5 mm
they look like a parachute and are usually split into two smaller droplets

large +

SNOW

When temperatures drop below 32°F (0°C), rain droplets freeze and form fluffy white snowflakes. These come in a variety of sizes and an infinite number of shapes.

Some are simple, shaped like a needle or a hexagon, but others have very intricate patterns and designs that make them spectacular, especially when viewed under a microscope.

They can be made up of 200 ice crystals. Snowflakes are exposed to a range of different weather conditions, and this is why almost every snowflake looks different.

The heaviest snowfall ever recorded was in the United States, on Mount Rainier in Washington State; 102 feet (31.1 m) of snow fell between February 19, 1971, and February 18, 1972.

102 ft (31.1 m)

The largest snowflake ever recorded was 15 in (38 cm) wide.

HAIL

Violent thunderstorms can produce hail. The water droplets inside the cloud are pushed toward the top where it is colder, as low as -4°F (-20°C), and they freeze to form ice particles. These start moving up and down through the storm, getting bigger and bigger as more droplets freeze to them, adding another layer to the hailstones. When they get too heavy to be supported by the updraft, the hailstones fall to the ground.

Sleet is different from snow. It's made up of small ice pellets that form when raindrops freeze as they fall.

The largest recorded hailstone weighed almost 4.4 lbs (2 kg), which is the same weight as a stone marten, a type of weasel. It fell in Kazakhstan, in Asia.

LIGHTNING

Lightning often occurs during a thunderstorm. **LIGHTNING** is an electric current. Inside the storm cloud, lots of small bits of ice bump into each other as they move around in the air, causing an electric charge. After a while, the entire cloud fills with electrical charges.

Negative charges are located in the bottom of the cloud. This causes an opposite, or positive, charge to build up on the ground beneath the cloud, which concentrates around anything that sticks up (steeples, trees, people). The charge coming up from these points connects with a charge reaching down from the cloud, and that's when lightning strikes!

While **LIGHTNING** is something we can see, **THUNDER** is something we hear, and it is one of the loudest sounds in nature. Thunder is created when the electrical discharge, or lightning, passes through the air and heats it rapidly.

We see the flash of lightning before we hear the thunder because light travels faster than sound!

About 1,000 lightning bolts strike Earth's surface every day, and there are millions of lightning storms every year. In an atmospheric electrical discharge, a bolt of lightning is roughly as hot as the surface of the sun (54,000°F/30,000°C) and can travel at speeds of 196,850 ft/s (60,000 m/s).

1,000 lightning strikes per day

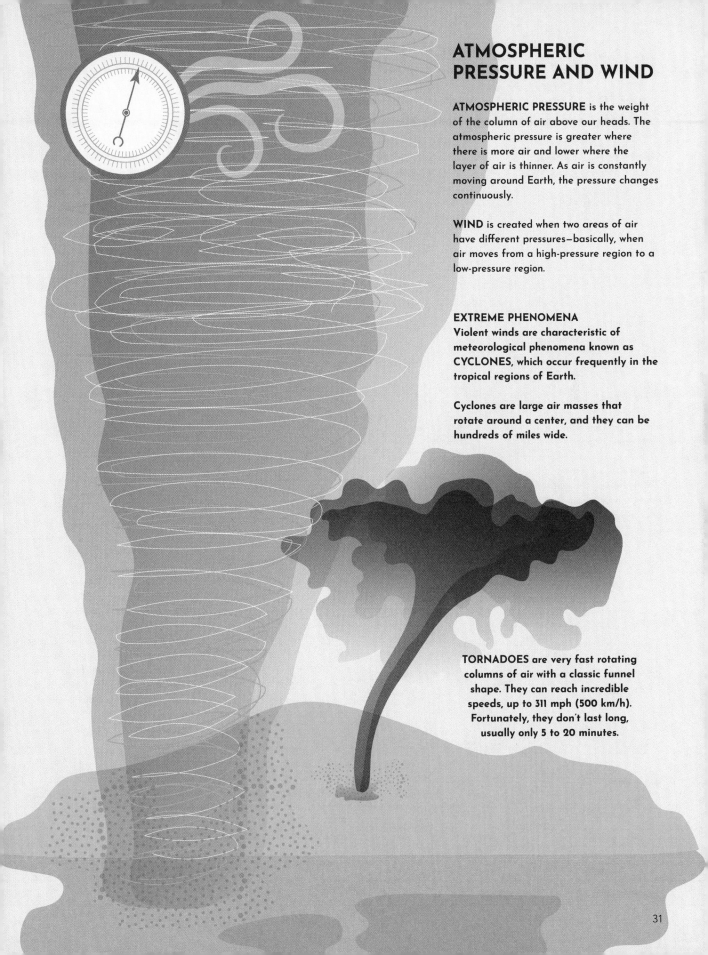

ATMOSPHERIC PRESSURE AND WIND

ATMOSPHERIC PRESSURE is the weight of the column of air above our heads. The atmospheric pressure is greater where there is more air and lower where the layer of air is thinner. As air is constantly moving around Earth, the pressure changes continuously.

WIND is created when two areas of air have different pressures—basically, when air moves from a high-pressure region to a low-pressure region.

EXTREME PHENOMENA
Violent winds are characteristic of meteorological phenomena known as **CYCLONES**, which occur frequently in the tropical regions of Earth.

Cyclones are large air masses that rotate around a center, and they can be hundreds of miles wide.

TORNADOES are very fast rotating columns of air with a classic funnel shape. They can reach incredible speeds, up to 311 mph (500 km/h). Fortunately, they don't last long, usually only 5 to 20 minutes.

AN OCEAN OF WATER

About 70% of our planet is covered with water.
Only 3% of this is fresh water, while the remaining 97% is salt water.

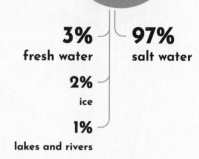

Most of Earth's fresh water is frozen in **ICE CAPS** and **GLACIERS**, while only a fraction of it is found in **LAKES** and **RIVERS**.

Salt water makes up the **OCEANS** and **SEAS**. It may seem strange, but less than 10% of these environments have been explored, even though we know they are there. This means that 90% of the world's oceans and seas have never been studied.

3%
fresh water

97%
salt water

2%
ice

1%
lakes and rivers

Salt in the ocean is mainly caused by rain transferring mineral salts from rocks on land into the water. These minerals have accumulated over millions of years, becoming more and more concentrated.

Underwater volcanoes and hydrothermal vents on the ocean floor can also release salts into the ocean.

"Normal" seawater

33.8 fl oz (1 liter)

Dead Sea water

33.8 fl oz (1 liter)

On average, 33.8 fl oz of seawater contains 1.2 ounces (35 g) of salt, but this can vary. A "closed" sea can become extra salty (called hypersaline) due to evaporation. The **DEAD SEA** is an example of this: 33.8 fl oz (1 liter) of water contains 11.3 oz (320 g) of salt. The high salt content causes the density of the water to increase, which is why a person can float more easily here than in other bodies of salt water.

11.3 oz (320 g) salt

1.2 oz (35 g) salt

OCEANS

The World Ocean is a continuous body of salt water that separates into oceans and seas. Conventionally, the larger bodies of salt water are called OCEANS.

1. Pacific Ocean

The Pacific Ocean is by far the largest ocean. It covers an area of approximately 60 million square miles (155 million km²) and contains more than half of the free water on Earth. It is so big that all of the world's continents could fit into it. It was named the Pacific (meaning "peaceful") by the explorer Ferdinand Magellan because the water was calm when he sailed across it. In reality, typhoons often occur in this ocean, and there are numerous active volcanoes in its basin. Earthquakes also occur frequently.

2. Atlantic Ocean

The Atlantic Ocean, whose name derives from that of the mythological god Atlas, is the second largest ocean; it's about half the size of the Pacific Ocean and covers 20% of Earth's surface. It separates the continents of North and South America from Europe and Africa. The longest mountain range on Earth runs along the Atlantic Ocean floor, stretching about 6,200 miles (10,000 km) from Iceland to Antarctica. It's called the Mid-Atlantic Ridge.

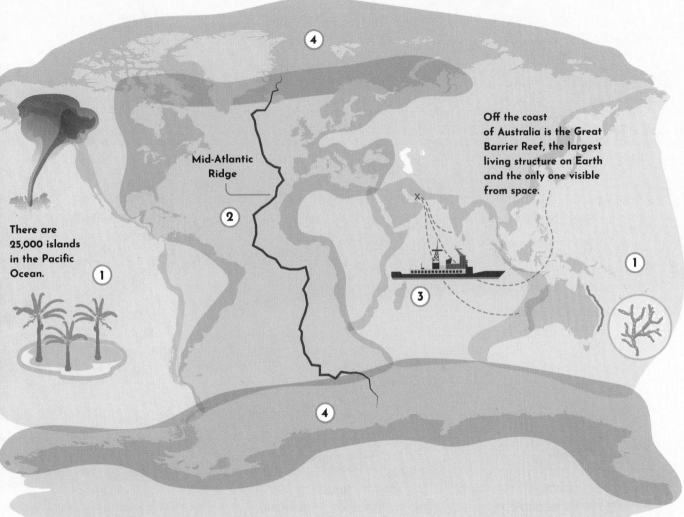

4

Mid-Atlantic Ridge

2

Off the coast of Australia is the Great Barrier Reef, the largest living structure on Earth and the only one visible from space.

There are 25,000 islands in the Pacific Ocean.

1

1

3

4

3. Indian Ocean

The Indian Ocean covers about 14% of Earth's surface and is located between Africa and South Asia. It's one of the most important oil shipping routes, as it connects the Middle Eastern countries, where oil is extracted, with Asia. Oil tankers coming from the Persian Gulf transport a total of 17 million barrels of crude oil per day.

4. Arctic Ocean and Southern Ocean

The Arctic Ocean and the Southern Ocean sit at opposite poles. The Arctic Ocean covers the North Pole, and in winter it's almost completely covered by sea ice. The Southern Ocean, which surrounds Antarctica, isn't considered a true ocean by many scientists, but rather the southernmost part of the larger oceans.

OCEAN FLOORS

Contrary to popular belief, ocean floors are not flat.
There is an extraordinary variety of landscapes, with mountains, valleys, and canyons, very similar to those we are used to seeing on land.

The ocean floor gently slopes along the continental shelf from the coast and then drops off steeply to form the continental slope. This is the true edge of the continent.

At the foot of the slope, which is about 13,000-20,000 ft (4,000-6,000 m) deep, there is a flat area that constitutes 40% of the oceans' floors. It is called an abyssal plain. These plains can be interrupted by features like mountain ranges, volcanic structures, and trenches.

Continental shelf

Continental slope

OCEAN MOVEMENTS

Ocean water never stops moving, but there are different types of motion. Here are the most common.

WAVES
Waves are the most typical type of movement in ocean water. There are many types of **WAVES**, but the ones we commonly see at the beach are created by the wind. The friction from the wind causes the surface water to move in ripples. If the wind keeps blowing, the waves get bigger and bigger. Waves look as if they're moving forward, but it is actually the energy that moves forward.

TIDES
The sea level changes during the day due to a phenomenon called the **TIDE**, for which the moon is mainly responsible. As our satellite orbits Earth, its gravity attracts ocean water toward it like a magnet. This means that the water level rises on the side of Earth closest to the moon, sometimes by more than 33 ft (10 m), while on the two sides perpendicular to the moon, the water level falls.

CURRENTS
Water in the ocean never stays in the same place but moves and flows continuously, forming **CURRENTS**. Ocean surface currents are driven by wind and tides, and when the wind changes direction, so can the flow of water. Deep-ocean currents, on the other hand, are caused by changes in the temperature, density, and salinity of the water.

34

Coral reefs are made up of 400 coral species and are home to over 2,000 species of fish, 4,000 mollusk species, and countless other invertebrates.

The deepest point known on Earth is in the Pacific Ocean, at the bottom of the Mariana Trench, and it's called the CHALLENGER DEEP. According to the last official survey carried out on December 7, 2011, it is located at 36,069.5 ft (10,994 m) below sea level.

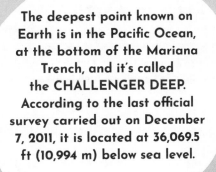

0 ft
(0 m)

820-1,640 ft
(250-500 m)

Abyssal plain

Mountain range

13,000-
20,000 ft
(4,000-6,000 m)

Ocean trench

32,800 ft
(10,000 m)

ANIMALS AND PLANTS

The ocean is a varied environment, where plants and animals have adapted very differently. It is estimated that there are approximately 250,000 species of creatures living in this immense environment, but, according to many scientists, there are definitely more! In unexplored waters, there are most certainly marine life-forms that have yet to be discovered—some estimate that there could be more than 25 million of them.

Life in the ocean mainly depends on two factors: light and pressure.

Light can only penetrate the water to a depth of a few thousand feet. Therefore, deeper down it is completely dark. The ocean is divided into three zones, based on the amount of light:

- 0-656 ft (0-200 m) > the euphotic zone: it is very light, and algae and plants can grow there.
- 656-3,280 ft (200-1,000 m) > the disphotic zone: here the light decreases rapidly with depth. Photosynthetic organisms are unable to live there.
- Deeper than 3,280 ft (1,000 m) > the aphotic zone: this represents about 90% of the ocean's volume. It is pitch black, and many of the animals living there have luminous organs.

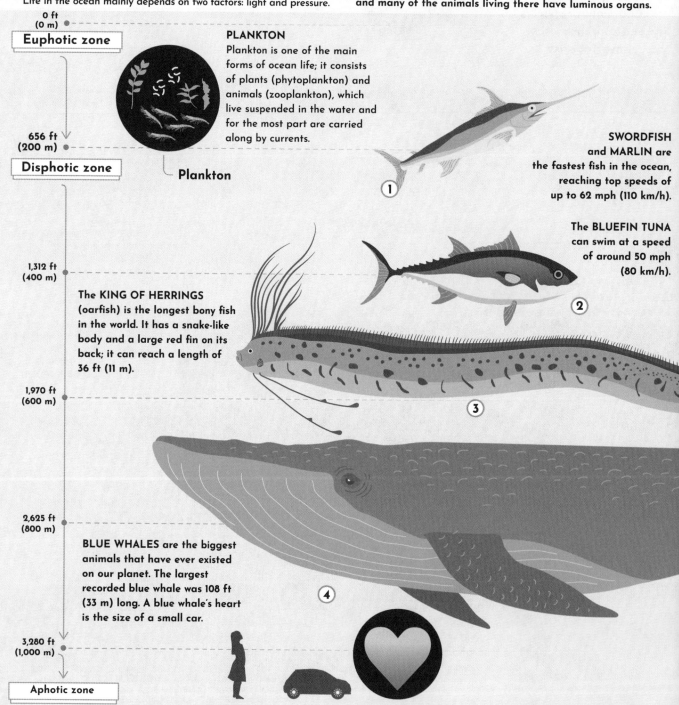

0 ft (0 m)

Euphotic zone

656 ft (200 m)

Disphotic zone

1,312 ft (400 m)

1,970 ft (600 m)

2,625 ft (800 m)

3,280 ft (1,000 m)

Aphotic zone

PLANKTON
Plankton is one of the main forms of ocean life; it consists of plants (phytoplankton) and animals (zooplankton), which live suspended in the water and for the most part are carried along by currents.

Plankton

SWORDFISH and **MARLIN** are the fastest fish in the ocean, reaching top speeds of up to 62 mph (110 km/h).
①

The **BLUEFIN TUNA** can swim at a speed of around 50 mph (80 km/h)
②

The **KING OF HERRINGS** (oarfish) is the longest bony fish in the world. It has a snake-like body and a large red fin on its back; it can reach a length of 36 ft (11 m).
③

BLUE WHALES are the biggest animals that have ever existed on our planet. The largest recorded blue whale was 108 ft (33 m) long. A blue whale's heart is the size of a small car.
④

36

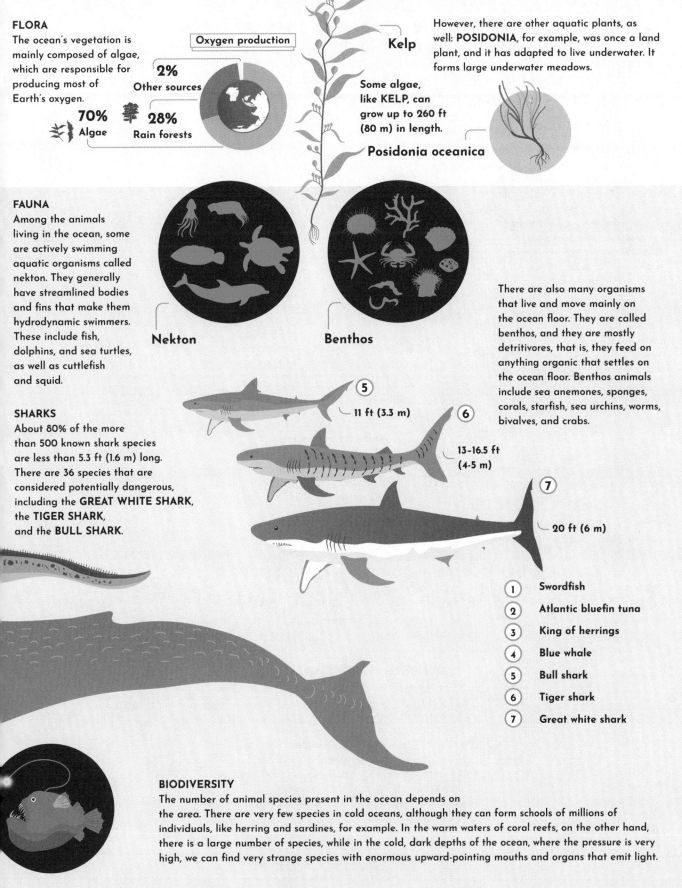

FLORA

The ocean's vegetation is mainly composed of algae, which are responsible for producing most of Earth's oxygen.

Oxygen production

2% Other sources

70% Algae

28% Rain forests

Kelp

Some algae, like KELP, can grow up to 260 ft (80 m) in length.

Posidonia oceanica

However, there are other aquatic plants, as well: POSIDONIA, for example, was once a land plant, and it has adapted to live underwater. It forms large underwater meadows.

FAUNA

Among the animals living in the ocean, some are actively swimming aquatic organisms called nekton. They generally have streamlined bodies and fins that make them hydrodynamic swimmers. These include fish, dolphins, and sea turtles, as well as cuttlefish and squid.

Nekton

Benthos

There are also many organisms that live and move mainly on the ocean floor. They are called benthos, and they are mostly detritivores, that is, they feed on anything organic that settles on the ocean floor. Benthos animals include sea anemones, sponges, corals, starfish, sea urchins, worms, bivalves, and crabs.

SHARKS

About 80% of the more than 500 known shark species are less than 5.3 ft (1.6 m) long. There are 36 species that are considered potentially dangerous, including the **GREAT WHITE SHARK**, the **TIGER SHARK**, and the **BULL SHARK**.

5 11 ft (3.3 m)

6 13-16.5 ft (4-5 m)

7 20 ft (6 m)

1. Swordfish
2. Atlantic bluefin tuna
3. King of herrings
4. Blue whale
5. Bull shark
6. Tiger shark
7. Great white shark

BIODIVERSITY

The number of animal species present in the ocean depends on the area. There are very few species in cold oceans, although they can form schools of millions of individuals, like herring and sardines, for example. In the warm waters of coral reefs, on the other hand, there is a large number of species, while in the cold, dark depths of the ocean, where the pressure is very high, we can find very strange species with enormous upward-pointing mouths and organs that emit light.

AT HIGH ALTITUDES

One-fifth of the world's landscape is occupied by mountains, although we can't see many of them because they are underwater, on the ocean floor.

Above ground, a mountain is any natural elevation higher than 1,968 ft (600 m) above sea level. A mountain usually has a base, called the **FOOTHILLS**, and **SLOPES** ranging from gentle to steep. Its highest point is called the **PEAK** or **SUMMIT**. There may be a **GLACIER** at the top, where there is perennial snow due to the very low temperatures.

Peak or Summit

Glacier

Slope

Pass

1,968 ft (600 m) ASL

Foot

An isolated group of mountains is called a **MASSIF**.

Valley

However, they are more commonly found in a row. These continuous series of aligned mountains are called **MOUNTAIN RANGES**.

4,660 mi (7,500 km)
The Andes

1,491 mi (2,400 km)
Himalayas

India

South America

HOW MOUNTAINS ARE FORMED

Mountains can be formed by volcanic activity, but they are more commonly created by the movements of Earth's crust.

A mountain range is formed when two tectonic plates smash into each other and buckle up, pushing huge slabs of rock to the surface. This is how the Himalayas began 55 million years ago, and today the range includes 30 of the world's highest mountains.

Because the plates beneath India and Asia are still pushing against each other, the Himalayas continue to rise a few millimeters every year!

Mt. Everest
Asia
29,028 ft (8,848 m)

20,321.5 ft (6,194 m)

Denali
(Mt. McKinley)
North America

**22,841.2 ft
(6,962 m)**

Mt. Aconcagua
South America

**19,563.6 ft
(5,963 m)**

Mt. Kilimanjaro
Africa

**18,481 ft
(5,633 m)**

Mt. Elbrus
Europe

**16,863.5 ft
(5,140 m)**

Vinson Massif
Antarctica

16,502.6 ft (5,030 m)

Puncak Jaya
Oceania

YOUNG AND OLD MOUNTAIN RANGES

If the mountains in a range have steep slopes and high, pointed peaks, it's an indication that it's a "young" formation and probably still growing. Don't forget that a few dozen million years is young for a mountain!

Ranges with low, rounded mountains, on the other hand, are very old; over millions of years, the mountains are slowly worn away as the rock is eroded by rain, wind, ice, and gravity, shaping the slopes and reducing their height.

Youngest mountain range: the Andes

about 70 million years old

Oldest mountain range: the Appalachians

about 350 million years old

MOUNTAIN GLACIERS

At the highest point of a mountain, the temperature is very often close to the freezing point of water. It snows a lot, and the snow accumulates to form bowl-shaped hollows called cirques. If the snow doesn't melt completely during the summer, there is an accumulation—that is, a glacier is formed. If these conditions persist, the ice increases in size and thickness over hundreds of years.

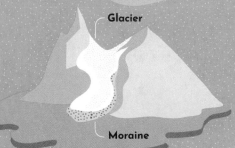

Glacier

Moraine

TERMINAL MORAINES

As glaciers begin to recede, they deposit their loads of rock, dirt, and gravel. These materials are called a moraine. Piles of moraine dumped at a glacier's end are called **TERMINAL MORAINES**.

THE MOVEMENT OF GLACIERS

Although a glacier may look like a solid block, it is actually moving very slowly under its own weight, causing it to slide downward. A glacier moves a few dozen feet a year, and new snow replaces the lost ice. Glaciers are extremely powerful. Like huge bulldozers, glaciers force their way through almost anything in their path. Clay, pebbles, and even boulders as large as houses are carried along by the ice for hundreds, even thousands, of miles.

CLIMATIC CONDITIONS

When you climb a mountain, the atmospheric temperature drops by about 32.9–34°F (0.5–0.6°C) every 328 feet (100 m), and it rains more often than at lower altitudes. The climate is influenced by latitude: In equatorial regions above 11,483 ft (3,500 m), ice can form any night of the year, but the heat then thaws it during the day.

Mountains at temperate latitudes have strongly marked seasons. In summer, the temperatures above the tree line are high enough for plants to grow for at least 100 days, while in winter, both days and nights are below freezing.

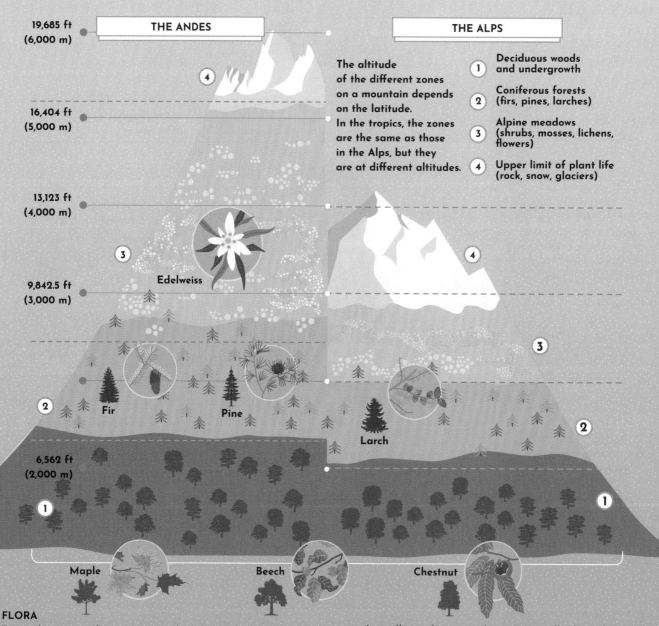

THE ANDES

THE ALPS

19,685 ft (6,000 m)

16,404 ft (5,000 m)

13,123 ft (4,000 m)

9,842.5 ft (3,000 m)

6,562 ft (2,000 m)

The altitude of the different zones on a mountain depends on the latitude. In the tropics, the zones are the same as those in the Alps, but they are at different altitudes.

1. Deciduous woods and undergrowth
2. Coniferous forests (firs, pines, larches)
3. Alpine meadows (shrubs, mosses, lichens, flowers)
4. Upper limit of plant life (rock, snow, glaciers)

Edelweiss

Fir

Pine

Larch

Maple

Beech

Chestnut

FLORA

Tropical mountain forests grow at the base of the mountain and are not found at higher latitudes. In temperate zones, the foothills are covered with deciduous woods, with trees that lose their leaves in winter and abundant undergrowth.

A little farther up, there are coniferous forests with firs, pines, and larches, and after that, beyond the tree line, there are much smaller and sparser plants. Eventually these disappear completely, giving way to alpine meadows with herbs, low-growing shrubs, mosses, and lichens.

Above a certain height, the vegetation stops: There is practically no soil, the air is constantly cold, there are very strong winds, and nothing grows. There is only rock partially covered by snow.

FAUNA

Mountains are not an easy environment to live in, especially for animals. The steep slopes are difficult to walk on; there are long, cold months with lots of snow; and there is a scarce supply of food. And if this weren't enough, as altitude increases, the air becomes thinner and it is more difficult to breathe. Yet, this habitat is home to a large number of species that exhibit unique adaptations.

The **GOLDEN EAGLE**, a majestic predator, dominates the skies over high mountains. The scarce vegetation on the peaks makes it easier for this bird to spot prey and swoop down to attack it.

The **SNOW LEOPARD** lives on the peaks of the Himalayas. Its stocky body and thick fur minimize heat loss, while its wide paws keep it from sinking into the snow.

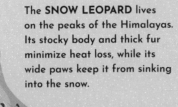

The **YAK**, a large bovine that lives on Asian mountains, can easily reach an altitude of 16,400 ft–19,700 ft (5,000–6,000 m). This is because it has a thick coat and also a very high number of red blood cells, which means it has no problem breathing at high altitudes, where the air is thin.

The Ethiopian Highlands are home to **GELADA** monkeys, which cope with the scarcity of nutritious food by eating the abundant grass. They use their hands to graze like herbivores.

Above 4,920 ft (1,500 m), the long, cold winters can be overcome by hibernating. This is what the alpine **MARMOT**—an animal typically found on European mountains—does, spending six months asleep in a burrow.

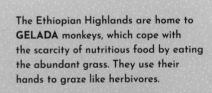

Climbing steep slopes can be difficult: Animals like **IBEX** or mountain goats have two toes that spread wide to improve balance.

The coat of the **STOAT** changes in winter. Its white winter coat helps it blend in with the snow, allowing it to both sneak up on prey and avoid becoming a meal itself!

FROM THE SOURCE TO THE RIVER MOUTH

Rivers and lakes are a source of fresh water that is essential for life on Earth, even though they contain less than 1% of the planet's water.

Over 80% of the world's fresh water comes from the mountains. The snow on the peaks melts in the summer, forming tiny streams that carry the water toward the ocean. Along the way, the streams collect snowmelt and rainfall runoff, both on the surface and in subsurface soil and rock.

HOW IS A RIVER FORMED?

The place where a river begins is called its **SOURCE**. It forms when the rainwater that has seeped deep into the ground finds a layer of impermeable rock, which it then flows over until it comes out of the ground. As it flows, the water carves out a groove in the soil, and over time this becomes its natural path.

80%
from the
mountains

Source

Permeable rock
Source
Impermeable
rock

Tributary

Delta

Estuary

A river's path starts from a high area and travels downward until it flows into a waterway or bed with embankments.

The waterways are very small at the source, but as they descend into the valley, they join each other and become bigger.

A freshwater stream that feeds into a larger river is called a **TRIBUTARY**.

CREEK
A creek is formed by the union of several streams. It is seasonal and may be dry at times.

STREAM
A stream is small and forms on the steepest slopes of a mountain. It can easily change course.

RIVER
A river can be very big. It is fed by several streams and is never dry.

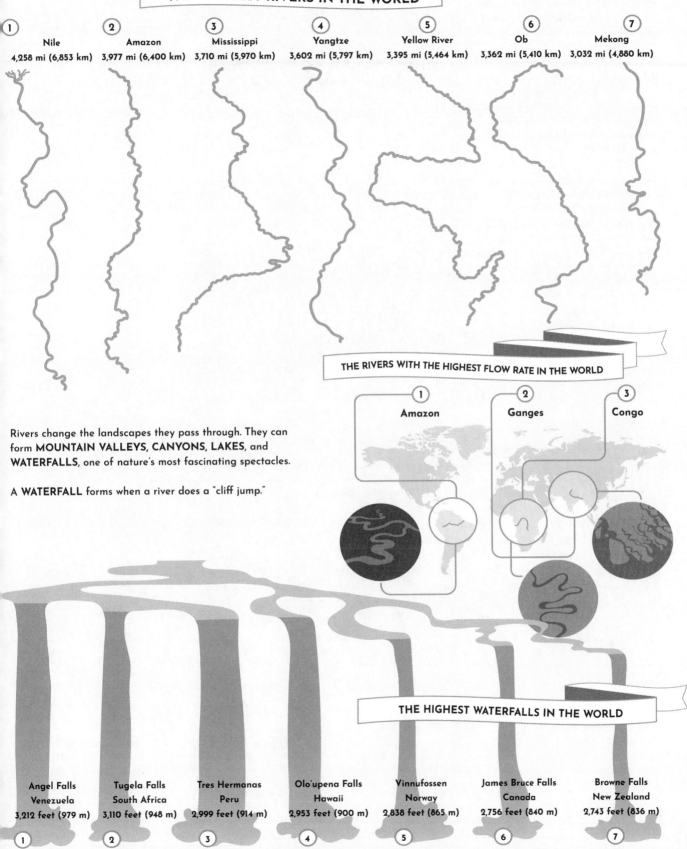

THE LONGEST RIVERS IN THE WORLD

① Nile	② Amazon	③ Mississippi	④ Yangtze	⑤ Yellow River	⑥ Ob	⑦ Mekong
4,258 mi (6,853 km)	3,977 mi (6,400 km)	3,710 mi (5,970 km)	3,602 mi (5,797 km)	3,395 mi (5,464 km)	3,362 mi (5,410 km)	3,032 mi (4,880 km)

Rivers change the landscapes they pass through. They can form **MOUNTAIN VALLEYS, CANYONS, LAKES,** and **WATERFALLS,** one of nature's most fascinating spectacles.

A **WATERFALL** forms when a river does a "cliff jump."

THE RIVERS WITH THE HIGHEST FLOW RATE IN THE WORLD

① Amazon	② Ganges	③ Congo

THE HIGHEST WATERFALLS IN THE WORLD

Angel Falls Venezuela	Tugela Falls South Africa	Tres Hermanas Peru	Olo'upena Falls Hawaii	Vinnufossen Norway	James Bruce Falls Canada	Browne Falls New Zealand
3,212 feet (979 m)	3,110 feet (948 m)	2,999 feet (914 m)	2,953 feet (900 m)	2,838 feet (865 m)	2,756 feet (840 m)	2,743 feet (836 m)
①	②	③	④	⑤	⑥	⑦

43

The type of erosion carried out by rivers is called **ABRASION**. Rivers are deepest in the middle of the riverbed, where the current is strongest, thanks to this erosion.

When the river reaches flat land, the water flows slowly because there is less of a slope. The river then becomes more sinuous, and lots of curves develop. These are called **LOOPS** or **MEANDERS**.

The quantities of water carried by rivers can vary greatly.

This quantity is called **FLOW RATE**, and it is measured by calculating how many cubic feet per second pass a particular point in a waterway. Generally, the flow of water in a river is not constant but varies over the seasons, depending on the amount of rainfall and how much snow melts on glaciers.

The water level of a river can therefore alternate between low and high.

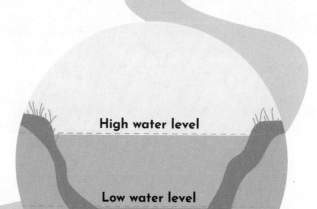

Loop or meander

High water level

Low water level

LAKES

When a river flows through a natural depression in Earth's surface, called a basin, it can fill it with water to form a lake. A river that flows into a lake is called a **TRIBUTARY**, while a river that flows out of it is called a **DISTRIBUTARY**. A lake can also form when a barrier, such as a landslide, blocks the course of a river. This type of lake disappears over time, filling up with sediment carried by the river. This reduces the depth, and vegetation slowly invades the area.

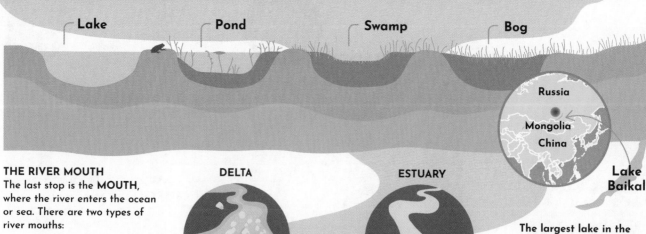

Lake   **Pond**   **Swamp**   **Bog**

Russia

Mongolia

China

Lake Baikal

THE RIVER MOUTH
The last stop is the **MOUTH**, where the river enters the ocean or sea. There are two types of river mouths:

DELTA

The river divides into lots of smaller branches, which flow over deposits of debris left by the river itself.

ESTUARY

Before it reaches the ocean, the river widens out in a funnel shape.

The largest lake in the world is Lake Baikal in Siberia. With a maximum depth of 5,387 feet (1,642 m), it is also the deepest lake on the planet.

FLORA AND FAUNA

The vegetation found in rivers mainly consists of aquatic plants and algae. Reeds are abundant where the river is calm. **CATTAILS** and **BULRUSHES** grow in the riverbed, but their stems and flowers stick out above the water.

1. Nile crocodile
2. Hippopotamus
3. Boto
4. Water lily
5. Hyacinth
6. Trout
7. Catfish
8. Gray heron
9. Bulrushes
10. Cattails
11. Mallard

Some plants, like water **LILIES** and **HYACINTHS**, have floating leaves and very beautiful flowers. Plants that prefer moist soil, like willows and poplars, grow on the river banks. Rivers are home to all kinds of animals: insects, crustaceans, amphibians, birds, reptiles, mammals, and over 10,000 species of fish.

One of the strangest animals in the world lives in the Amazon River: It is called a **BOTO**, or pink river dolphin, and it is a freshwater cetacean that can reach a length of 10 feet (3 m).

TROUT prefer the choppy water of streams, where the continuous movement of the water guarantees a high concentration of oxygen. Carps and **CATFISH**, on the other hand, prefer calmer waters.

The **HIPPOPOTAMUS** spends the hot hours of the day in water, with only its ears, eyes, and nose above the water, all of which are at the top of its head. It closes its nostrils and ears when it dives.

The Nile **CROCODILE** is the most fearsome reptile of all. Despite its size (up to 20 ft/6m long), it is very good at hiding because its coloration provides camouflage, and it can remain motionless for long periods, almost totally submerged.

Many birds live on the banks of waterways and lakes, where they build nests, often hidden in places protected by vegetation. Some, like ducks and **MALLARDS**, have webbed feet for swimming and diving, while others, such as **HERONS**, flamingos, and cranes, have long legs so they can walk in the water without getting wet.

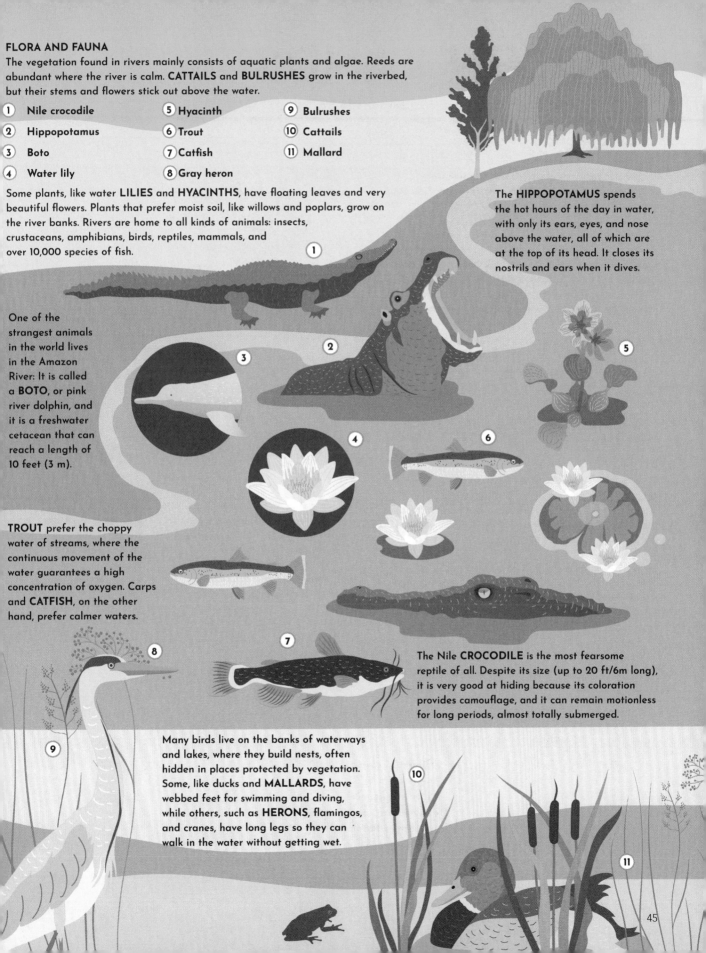

45

FROZEN LANDS

The Arctic and Antarctica are the two ends of the world. They are called Earth's poles.

The name "Arctic" comes from the Greek word *arktos*, meaning "bear." It refers to the constellation Ursa Major, or Great Bear, which appears in the northern sky. Antarctica simply means "opposite to the bear."

Due to their position, the **POLES** are the coldest places on the planet. The sun is always low on the horizon, and its rays hit the ground at a lower angle, therefore reducing the heat. Furthermore, because Earth's axis is tilted, the sun stays above the horizon for months on end, without ever setting, while there are other months when it doesn't rise at all.

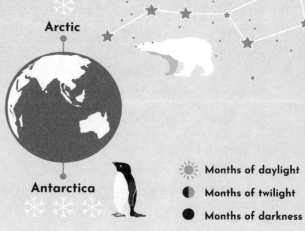

Arctic

Antarctica

☀ Months of daylight
◑ Months of twilight
● Months of darkness

	JAN	FEB	MAR	APR	MAY	JUN	JUL	AUG	SEPT	OCT	NOV	DEC
NORTH POLE	●	●	◑	☀	☀	☀	☀	☀	◑	●	●	●
SOUTH POLE	☀	☀	◑	●	●	●	●	●	◑	☀	☀	☀

There are differences between the two poles. For starters, the South Pole is much colder. This is because of the geographic differences between the Arctic and Antarctic; the Arctic is an ocean surrounded by continents, while Antarctica is a true continent, surrounded by an ocean.

Despite the large amount of ice, Antarctica is a dry and arid region and is considered a desert. Precipitation here is rare, mostly in the form of snow, amounting to just 2 in (5 cm) a year.

More than 98% of Antarctica is covered by a sheet of ice, called an ice cap, with an average thickness of a little over 1.3 mi (2.2 km), although in some inland areas it can reach 3 mi (5 km) thick.

Violent, cold winds blow down from the slopes, reaching speeds of 186.5 mph (300 km/h), that sweep across this wasteland.

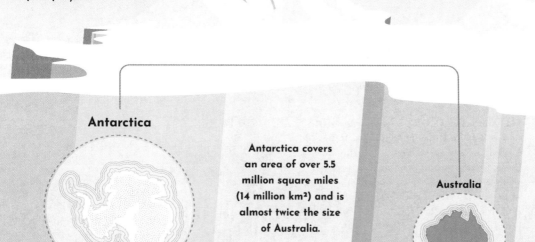

Antarctica

Antarctica covers an area of over 5.5 million square miles (14 million km²) and is almost twice the size of Australia.

Australia

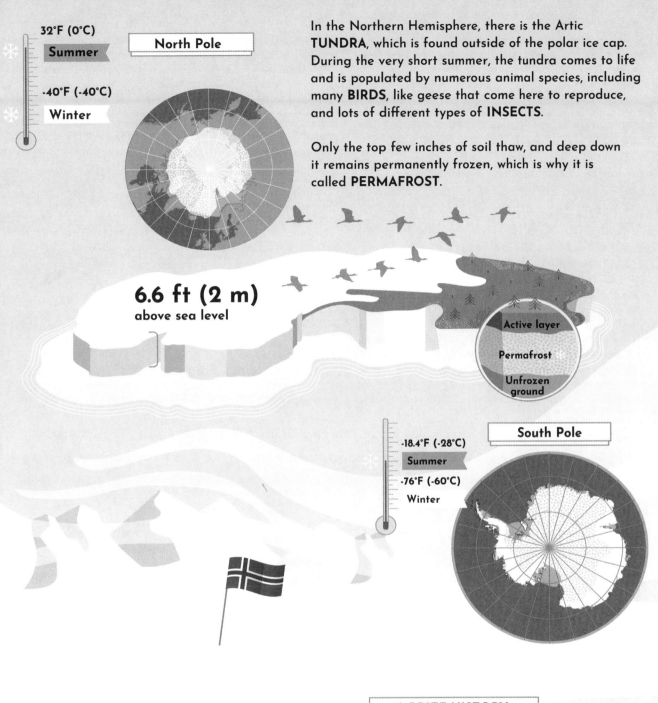

32°F (0°C)
Summer

-40°F (-40°C)
Winter

North Pole

In the Northern Hemisphere, there is the Artic **TUNDRA**, which is found outside of the polar ice cap. During the very short summer, the tundra comes to life and is populated by numerous animal species, including many **BIRDS**, like geese that come here to reproduce, and lots of different types of **INSECTS**.

Only the top few inches of soil thaw, and deep down it remains permanently frozen, which is why it is called **PERMAFROST**.

6.6 ft (2 m)
above sea level

Active layer

Permafrost

Unfrozen ground

-18.4°F (-28°C)
Summer

-76°F (-60°C)
Winter

South Pole

A BRIEF HISTORY

Antarctica contains about 70% of Earth's fresh water and about 90% of its ice.

The first person to cross Antarctica and reach the South Pole was the Norwegian explorer Roald Amundsen. With a team of just four men, he traveled for 57 days on sleds pulled by 52 dogs, arriving at his destination on December 14, 1911.

The first person to reach the "roof of the world," however, has been a long-standing controversy. Two American explorers both claimed to have discovered the North Pole, each saying that the other was a fraud. Robert Peary said he reached the North Pole on April 6, 1909, while Frederick Cook said he had accomplished the feat a year earlier, on April 21, 1908. To date, neither of the two claims have been proved with 100% certainty.

VEGETATION

The freezing temperatures and long periods of darkness mean that it is difficult for terrestrial plants to survive at the poles, as there is no soil for the roots and, above all, no light for photosynthesis.

Only during the short thaw season in the Artic **TUNDRA**, in the Northern Hemisphere, is it possible to find many species of low-growing grasses, mosses, lichens, and small shrubs.

It is a different story in the ocean. There is an abundance of microscopic algae that form large phytoplankton blooms. Algae are what krill feed on, and these crustaceans are a very important link in the food webs in the polar regions. It is estimated that 500 million tons of krill live in the Southern Ocean, making it the most abundant animal on the planet.

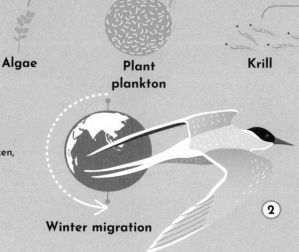

Algae

Plant plankton

Krill

Winter migration

ANIMALS IN THE ARCTIC

There are several land animals that live in the Arctic, both on the sea ice and, more commonly, in the tundra: reindeer and caribou, musk oxen, lemmings, arctic hares, arctic wolves, arctic foxes, and polar bears.

Birds include **SNOWY OWLS** and **ARCTIC TERNS**, which have the longest migration of all: During the winter, arctic terns fly over 27,962 mi (45,000 km) to Antarctica, on the opposite side of the world, in just less than four months.

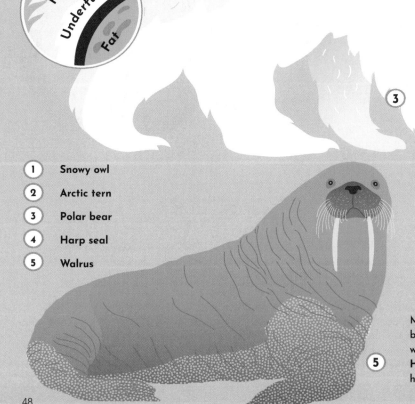

Fur

Underfur

Fat

The **POLAR BEAR** is the undisputed king of the Arctic. To withstand the low temperatures, polar bears have two layers of fur and a layer of fat under the skin. Their skin is black, and their hairs are hollow, allowing them to absorb as much heat as possible from the sunlight.

1. Snowy owl
2. Arctic tern
3. Polar bear
4. Harp seal
5. Walrus

Many animals live in the sea, including some really big ones: **WALRUSES**, narwhals, beluga whales, arctic whales, and numerous species of seals (bearded seals, **HARP SEALS**, ribbon seals, ringed seals, hooded seals, harbor seals, spotted seals, gray seals).

ANIMALS IN ANTARCTICA

It may seem strange, but the largest strictly terrestrial animal in Antarctica is an insect, the **BELGIAN GNAT** (*Belgica antarctica*), which is less than 0.5 in (1 cm) long. It doesn't have wings, which prevents it from being blown away by strong winds.

Belgian gnat
< 0.5 in/1 cm (1:1 scale)

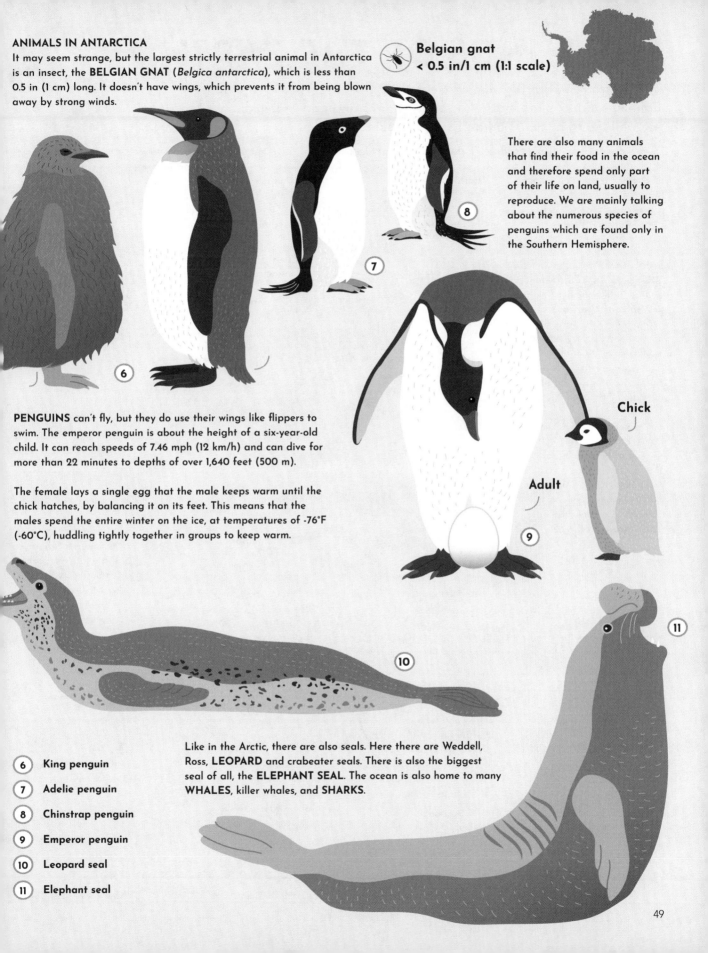

There are also many animals that find their food in the ocean and therefore spend only part of their life on land, usually to reproduce. We are mainly talking about the numerous species of penguins which are found only in the Southern Hemisphere.

PENGUINS can't fly, but they do use their wings like flippers to swim. The emperor penguin is about the height of a six-year-old child. It can reach speeds of 7.46 mph (12 km/h) and can dive for more than 22 minutes to depths of over 1,640 feet (500 m).

The female lays a single egg that the male keeps warm until the chick hatches, by balancing it on its feet. This means that the males spend the entire winter on the ice, at temperatures of -76°F (-60°C), huddling tightly together in groups to keep warm.

Chick

Adult

Like in the Arctic, there are also seals. Here there are Weddell, Ross, **LEOPARD** and crabeater seals. There is also the biggest seal of all, the **ELEPHANT SEAL**. The ocean is also home to many **WHALES**, killer whales, and **SHARKS**.

(6) **King penguin**

(7) **Adelie penguin**

(8) **Chinstrap penguin**

(9) **Emperor penguin**

(10) **Leopard seal**

(11) **Elephant seal**

THE LUNGS OF THE EARTH

Defining a forest as a group of trees that grow together is far too simplistic. Forests are essential to our planet and generally contribute to the well-being of all its inhabitants, including humans.

Forests absorb carbon dioxide and other greenhouse gases, which are responsible for global warming, from the atmosphere, thereby preventing climate change.

Furthermore, they contain billions of trees and are home to 80% of the world's terrestrial biodiversity and countless species of animals and plants, many of which are yet to be discovered.

There are several types of forests, and each has its own distinctive characteristics, depending on its distance from the equator, the soil it grows in, and the climatic conditions of its region.

31%
of Earth's land surface is covered by forests

RAIN FORESTS

These grow across the equator and up to the tropics of both hemispheres. They can be found in South America, Africa, and Southeast Asia. They have the highest diversity of animal and plant species—there are millions of species, at least half of all those on the planet.

The largest is the Amazon rain forest, which is almost half the size of Europe. To date, 350 mammal species, 3,000 fish species, 1,000 bird species, 3,000 plant species, and 10,000 species of invertebrates have been discovered there.

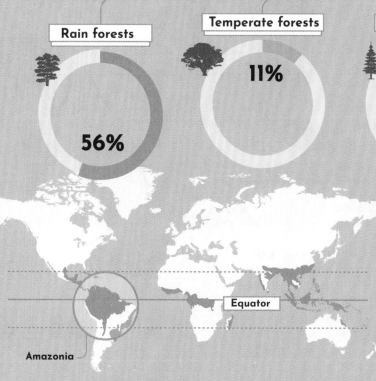

Rain forests

56%

Temperate forests

11%

Boreal forests

33%

80.6°F (27°C)

Equator

Amazonia

In a rain forest, the temperature is stable all year round at about 80.6°F (27°C). The plants get a lot of water because it rains often, sometimes every day.

FLORA AND FAUNA

The trees in a rain forest can reach dizzying heights. There are a number of clear layers of vegetation, and although most of the animals are arboreal (live in the trees), there is fauna everywhere.

Emergent layer

Up here there is a lot of sunlight, but only the tops of the tallest trees, which can be up to 164-197 ft (50-60 m) high, can reach it.

Canopy

This is the main layer of the forest and it forms a roof over the area below. It is made up of trees that are up to 65.6 ft (20 m) tall, which form a labyrinth of branches, made even more intricate by hanging vines.

Understory

This layer is in the shade constantly, so the plants have large leaves in order to capture the scarce sunlight. Many of these, such as orchids and bromeliads, are epiphytes, that is, they grow on trees and obtain water with their aerial roots.

Floor

Only 1% of the sun's rays reach the floor, and so it is very dark here. This means that there are no plants and the animals include lots of insects.

1. Harpy eagle
2. Blue morpho
3. Vampire bat

4. Tree boa
5. Sloth
6. Orangutan
7. Toco toucan
8. Scarlet macaw

9. Jaguar
10. Poison arrow frog

11. Leaf-cutter ant
12. Puma
13. South American tapir

THE RAIN FOREST

Emergent layer

164 ft
(50 m)

98.5 ft
(30 m)

Canopy

65.6 ft
(20 m)

Understory

33 ft
(10 m)

0 ft
(0 m)

Floor

TEMPERATE FORESTS

Temperate forests are found in mid-latitude regions, mainly in the Northern Hemisphere, where rainfall is abundant all year round and there are four well-defined seasons.

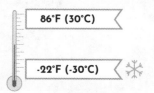

86°F (30°C)

-22°F (-30°C)

Equator

In general, the temperature varies from -22°F to 86°F (-30 to 30°C), and average yearly precipitation is 30-60 in (75-150 cm).

Mainly deciduous trees grow in temperate forests, such as oaks, beeches, maples, elms, birches, chestnuts, and walnuts. On average, there are 3-4 tree species per square mile. In fall, the leaves on these trees turn beautiful shades of orange, yellow, and red before falling to the ground.

The leaves have to fall off because the water inside the cells could freeze in the cold weather, seriously damaging the plant. The fallen leaves then decompose, and combined with the moderate temperatures, this makes the soil very fertile.

When the temperatures drop and the hours of daylight decrease, the chlorophyll in the leaves breaks down and photosynthesis stops.

The green color disappears and is replaced with shades of orange and yellow.

The tree then blocks the passage of sugar through the leaf, so it builds up in the leaf's cells and produces a red pigment.

A temperate forest has only two layers of vegetation. The branches and leaves of the tallest trees make up the canopy, which can reach a height of 49-98.5 ft (15-30 m). Below this is the understory, which is composed of lower plants.

There are always **FERNS**, **MOSSES**, and **LICHENS** in the understory, which are able to survive even in summer when they receive only a little sunlight.

(1) Red fox

(2) Wild boar

(3) Common badger

(4) Common hare

(5) Grey wolf

(6) American elk

(7) Great spotted woodpecker

(8) Eurasian jay

(9) Eurasian golden oriole

THE TEMPERATE FOREST

98.5 ft
(30 m)

9

82 ft
(25 m)

65.5 ft
(20 m)

8

Canopy

49 ft
(15 m)

7

6

33 ft
(10 m)

3

16.5 ft
(5 m)

4

5

Understory

0 ft
(0 m)

53

BOREAL OR TAIGA FORESTS

In the Subarctic, an area of the Northern Hemisphere, the continents are covered with boreal forests, which are also known by their Russian name, TAIGA.

There are two seasons in a taiga forest: a short, humid, and mildly warm summer and a very long, cold, and snowy winter. There is only one thin layer of soil in a boreal forest, and it is poor in nutrients. Since the forest is mostly composed of evergreen plants, very little sunlight reaches the ground, so plant growth in the understory is very limited.

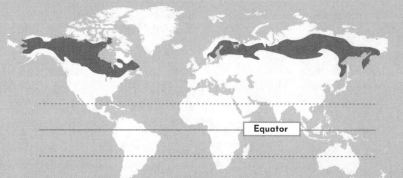

Equator

68°F (20°C)

-40°F (-40°C)

Temperatures range from -40°F to 68°F (-40°C to 20°C), and average yearly precipitation is 16-40 in (40-100 cm).

Taiga forests are home to conifers, such as **PINES, LARCHES,** and **FIRS,** which have characteristic needle-like leaves.

Many conifers are cone-shaped, with the tips of branches pointing upwards. This prevents snow from building up on the branches and breaking them.

Broad leaves

Needle-shaped leaves

BROAD LEAVES, NEEDLE-SHAPED LEAVES
Both types of leaves are organs that plants need for photosynthesis, and both can be food for a variety of other organisms.

They drop in the fall

Large surface area to absorb sunlight

They only photosynthesize in the summer

They sustain damage at low temperatures

They can lose a lot of water due to evaporation

They drop gradually every 3-4 years

Smaller surface area to absorb sunlight

They photosynthesize all year round

They can tolerate low temperatures

They have a cuticle that prevents water loss

FAUNA
Both temperate and boreal forests are home to many species of animals, including deer, badgers, wolves, wild boars, bears, moose, lynxes, hares, and birds, many of which only arrive in the summer for the breeding season.

Animals that hibernate:

SLEEP OR HIBERNATION?
The most difficult season for animals is winter, when food is scarce and temperatures drop below zero. This is why many species spend their days sleeping, but not all in the same way.

Dormice

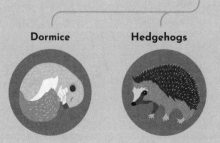

Hedgehogs

Bats

Reptiles

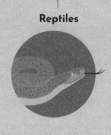

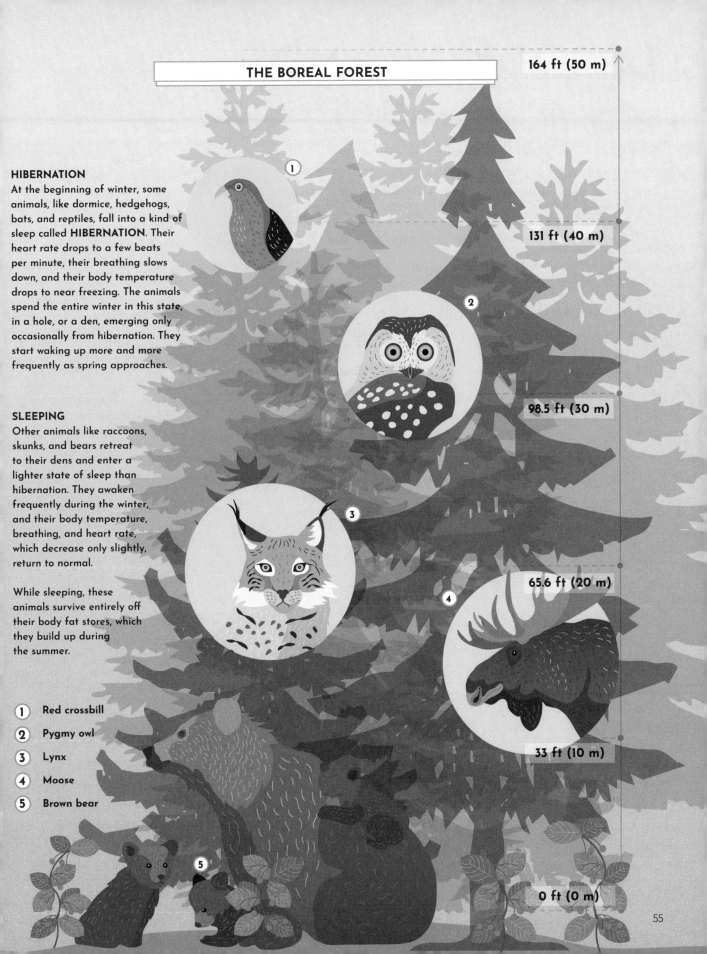

THE BOREAL FOREST

164 ft (50 m)

131 ft (40 m)

HIBERNATION

At the beginning of winter, some animals, like dormice, hedgehogs, bats, and reptiles, fall into a kind of sleep called **HIBERNATION**. Their heart rate drops to a few beats per minute, their breathing slows down, and their body temperature drops to near freezing. The animals spend the entire winter in this state, in a hole, or a den, emerging only occasionally from hibernation. They start waking up more and more frequently as spring approaches.

SLEEPING

Other animals like raccoons, skunks, and bears retreat to their dens and enter a lighter state of sleep than hibernation. They awaken frequently during the winter, and their body temperature, breathing, and heart rate, which decrease only slightly, return to normal.

While sleeping, these animals survive entirely off their body fat stores, which they build up during the summer.

98.5 ft (30 m)

65.6 ft (20 m)

33 ft (10 m)

(1) Red crossbill

(2) Pygmy owl

(3) Lynx

(4) Moose

(5) Brown bear

0 ft (0 m)

55

DESOLATE LANDS

A desert isn't determined by high temperatures or the number of organisms that live there, but by the low rainfall, which in some cases occurs only once every two or three years.

Deserts can either be hot, like the Sahara, the largest desert on the planet, or cold, like the Gobi Desert in Central Asia.

However, big differences in daily temperatures can also be recorded in hot deserts. While it can be very hot during the day, reaching as high as 122°F (50°C), at night under a cloudless sky, the ground quickly loses the accumulated heat and the temperature can drop below freezing. This difference is temperatures is called **TEMPERATURE RANGE**.

Cold desert

Hot desert

Deserts can be:

Extremely dry:
They have at least 12 consecutive months without rain.

Arid:
They have less than 10 in (250 mm) of rain per year.

Semiarid:
They have between 10 and 20 in (250-500 mm) of rain per year.

AROUND THE WORLD
The largest hot desert in the world is the Sahara, which covers most of North Africa and is the same size as China. The largest cold desert, not including the polar deserts in the Arctic and Antarctic, is the Gobi Desert, which extends into East Asia.

THE WORLD'S DESERTS

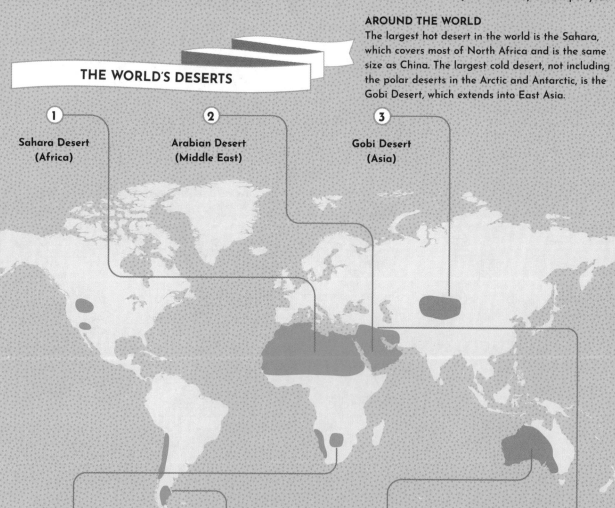

1 Sahara Desert (Africa)

2 Arabian Desert (Middle East)

3 Gobi Desert (Asia)

4 Kalahari Desert (Africa)

5 Patagonian Desert (South America)

6 Great Victoria Desert (Australia)

7 Syrian Desert (Middle East)

TYPES OF DESERTS

Sand deserts are without a doubt the most well known, but they are just one of many types of desert. Rocky and stony deserts are actually much more common.

These are formed by continuous wind erosion as well as by the daily temperature range. The rocks crumble continuously, breaking down into smaller and smaller pebbles, and eventually gravel.

Only 20% of Earth's deserts are sandy

Sandy deserts (called ERGS)

Stony deserts (called SERIR)

Rocky deserts (called HAMMADA)

DUNES AND OASES

DUNES are large mounds of sand formed by the wind. The wind makes the sand grains roll up the side of the dune on the leeward side. Once they reach the top, the grains fall down the other side, which is much steeper. This continuous movement of the grains causes the dune to grow up to several feet per year. The dunes grow to a maximum height of 1,640 feet (500 m).

OASES are isolated places in the desert that are surrounded by lush vegetation. An oasis forms when the water table rises to the surface. They are an important water supply for many animals, as well as for the nomadic tribes that live in these desolate places.

Why do deserts form?
There are several reasons: Some deserts form because a mountain range "blocks" the passage of humid air and consequently it hardly ever rains; others form in regions that are too far from the ocean to be reached by air currents containing moisture; or they form in areas where two dry air masses meet, causing long periods of drought.

The word "DESERT" comes from the Latin *desertus*, which means "abandoned." Actually, lots of plants, animals, and other organisms live in deserts, having adapted to survive in very difficult conditions, with scarcity of water and nutrient-poor soil.

FLORA

Many plants store water in their stems. They often have a very short life cycle, which only begins and ends when it rains.

WELWITSCHIA plants grow in the Namib Desert. On average, they are 500-600 years old, but there are some as old as 2,000 years. Their leaves grow all the time, just like hair!

The most common plants are EUPHORBIAS and CACTI, which are similar because they both adapt to the same environmental conditions. Both tend to have a lot of prickles, which are there to protect the plant. Euphorbias most often have thorns, whereas cacti have spines that are modified leaves.

CHARACTERISTICS OF CACTI

- Their surface is waxy to reduce the loss of water, and it is folded like an accordion so it can expand and act as a reservoir.

- Their stems and branches are fleshy so they can store water.

- Their leaves are pointed spines so as to reduce water loss, so photosynthesis occurs in the stem.

- Generally, they have amazing flowers that bloom at night, although they are short-lived.

- Their seeds are dormant for years and only sprout when it rains.

Cacti evolved in the New World, while euphorbias appeared in the Old World, spreading mainly to Africa, Madagascar, and the drier parts of Asia.

FAUNA

Like plants, desert animals have also developed many adaptive strategies for coping with the scarcity of water. In general, they get water from food and store it in their body without wasting it.

Herbivores, such as the **ADDAX ANTELOPE** and the **ORYX**, get water from the plants they eat and never need to drink it, while carnivores get fluids from the bodies of their prey.

In hot deserts, many animals are active at night, like the **KANGAROO RAT**, and they spend the sweltering hot days in underground burrows. At depths lower than 20 in (50 cm), the temperature remains around 86°F (30°C), regardless of how hot it is outside.

The **AFRICAN HORNED VIPER** has developed a way to move across the sand without sinking in it, moving sideways as if it were swimming.

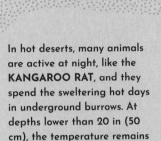

A **DROMEDARY CAMEL** minimizes its water loss by producing very concentrated urine and dry dung. It can also lose 40% of its body weight without dying of dehydration.

Dromedary

- It's taller than a bactrian (6.5 ft/2 m)
- Its coat is short
- It has only 1 hump
- It comes from the Arabian Peninsula (hot desert)

Bactrian

- It's smaller than a dromedary (5 ft/1.5 m)
- Its coat is long
- It has 2 humps
- It comes from Asia (hot desert)

A **BACTRIAN CAMEL** can survive without water for more than a week.

BACTRIAN AND DROMEDARY CAMELS ARE DESERT MAMMALS

To prevent getting sand in their eyes and noses, bactrian and dromedary camels have very long **EYELASHES** and can close their nostrils. Their **HUMPS** can store over 77 lbs (35 kg) of fat.

LIKE OCEANS OF GRASS

The word "savanna" generally indicates an open plain where grass grows abundantly and trees are fairly scarce and spaced widely apart.

About 20% of Earth's surface is covered by savannas.

The name "savanna" derives from the Taino word *zabana*. Taino is an ancient language that was spoken by American Indians on some of the Caribbean islands. It became part of the French, English, and Spanish languages between 1529 and 1555, when Europeans began exploring the Caribbean.

Although there are savannas on other continents, such as Asia and Australia, the largest in the world is in Africa. It covers some 5 million square miles (13 million km²), which is about half of the continent!

The name "savanna" derives from the Taino word *zabana*. Taino is an ancient language that was spoken by American Indians on some of the Caribbean islands. It became part of the French, English, and Spanish languages between 1529 and 1555, when Europeans began exploring the Caribbean.

Although there are savannas on other continents, such as Asia and Australia, the largest in the world is in Africa. It covers some 5 million square miles (13 million km²), which is about half of the continent!

Rainy season

Dry season

SAVANNAS are not all the same. First, they vary according to the length of the dry season and are therefore subdivided into three categories: wet, dry, and thornbush. Second, they are classified by the ratio of grass species to other plant species. So, there are also grassy savannas, shrub savannas, and tree or woodland savannas.

Unlike grasses, trees can only store water in their roots and produce leaves during the rainy season, when the slightly cooler temperature limits excessive transpiration.

The most common tree in the savanna is the **UMBRELLA THORN ACACIA**, which stores water in its bark. Its canopy is shaped like an umbrella, hence the name. It is a source of food for lots of animals, as well as a refuge for many birds. The acacia tree has developed several defense mechanisms to avoid losing its leaves: thorns, bitter-tasting leaves, and an "alliance" with ants!

Crowned crane

Umbrella thorn acacia

Secretary bird

50%
of the continent of Africa is covered by savannas.

68-86°F (20-30°C)

82 ft (25 m)

FLORA
A savanna is nothing more than a grassland with a few trees here and there. The long periods without water makes life difficult for very tall trees, which can only thrive if they are near ponds or waterways. Grasses are therefore the most abundant plants, as they are able to survive the high temperatures and long periods of drought during the dry season.

Savannas have warm climates: Temperatures are between 68 and 86°F (20°C-30°C), with only slight variations throughout the year.

Baobab

ACACIA ANTS
An acacia tree can host up to 30,000 ants, which drive away any animals trying to feed on the tree by biting and stinging them. They remove any fungi that are harmful to the tree and even go so far as to cut down other small plants that might compete with their tree for sunlight. So as not to lose these precious little helpers, the acacia tree produces a nectar that contains an enzyme, which prevents the ants from eating other sources of sugar. This means that if the ants leave the tree, they would starve.

Another very common species in this environment is the **BAOBAB** tree. Its swollen trunk can reach a height of 82 ft (25 m) and a diameter of 10-33 ft (3-10 m). The bark is compact and resinous, and the tree uses it to store water. It is also fire-resistant and prevents water from evaporating. Some of them are over a thousand years old.

FAUNA

The abundant vegetation means that there are plenty of herbivorous animals, which in turn feed a long series of carnivores, including many felines (such as lions, leopards, cheetahs, servals), canids (jackals, wild dogs), and hyenas. The most numerous herbivores are the antelopes. This group includes very different species.

Herbivores feed on plants, and all of them are able to live in the same environment because they share resources: They each have their own favorite food, and they feed on plants that are at different heights from the ground or at different times, depending on the time of year.

CARNIVORES

HERBIVORES

Felines

Leopards

Cheetahs

Lions

Canids

Wild dogs

Jackals

Hyenas

Antelopes

Elands

Gazelles

Gerenuks

Impalas

Kudus

Other herbivores

Buffaloes

Elephants

Warthogs

Giraffes

Gnus

Rhinoceroses

Zebras

1

LIONS can grow up to a length of 10 ft (3m)!

The CHEETAH is the fastest land animal in the world and can sprint at 68 mph (110 km/h) to catch its prey!

THE GREAT MIGRATION

In some regions of Africa at the beginning of the dry season, many herbivores migrate to other regions in search of water. Herds made up of millions of individuals of different species set off, walking for up to 500 mi (800 km). The females give birth to their young along the way. The journey presents dangers and difficulties, but the animals can rely on herd numbers and speed, especially in the vast open areas where predators launch their attacks.

CAMOUFLAGE AND MIMICRY

Predators often need to camouflage themselves, that is, to hide by blending in with their surroundings, so they can get as close as possible to their prey and catch them by surprise. This is why many felines have a spotted coat, as it blends perfectly with the shade, light, and shadows created on the ground by the sun's rays.

GIRAFFES are the tallest animals in the world, growing up to 20 ft (6m) tall!

ELEPHANTS are the largest land animals in the world.

1. Lion
2. African elephant
3. Giraffe
4. Warthog
5. Pangolin

TERMITE MOUNDS

The world's savannas are filled with **TERMITES**, social insects that, like ants, live in large groups and share the same nest called a **TERMITE MOUND**.

Termite mounds can be as high as 16.5 ft (5 m) and are a characteristic and very visible element in any savanna.

Termites are detritivorous insects, that is, they feed on rotten wood and plants, and they play an important role in soil formation. They are also a source of food for many animals, such as **PANGOLINS** and aardwolves.

16.5 ft (5 m)

THE DARK SIDE OF THE EARTH

A cave is a natural chamber, often located under the Earth's surface. Most of the time, caves are not a single chamber, but a complicated system of chambers connected to each other by underground tunnels.

The scientific study of caves and the surrounding environments is called **SPELEOLOGY**, and a speleologist is the person who explores caves to study them.

Cave systems can't be more than about 9,800 ft (3,000 m) beneath the surface. At greater depths, the weight of the overlying rocks would exert too much pressure, causing the structure to collapse.

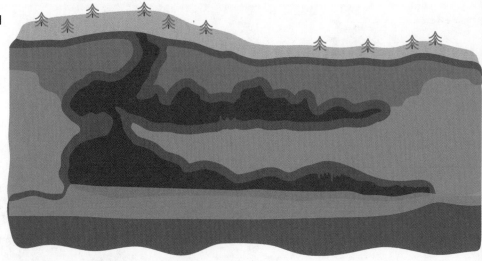

Caves can be formed in various ways, usually over millions of years.

THE MOST COMMON TYPES OF CAVES ARE:

CORRASIONAL CAVES
They are formed when carbon dioxide reacts with water seeping into the ground, forming an acid that dissolves particularly soluble rocks, such as limestone.

LAVA CAVES
They are formed by lava that cools and hardens on the surface, while the hot lava continues to flow below, leaving a cavity behind.

EROSIONAL CAVES
They are formed by the erosive action of wind, waves, and tides (sea caves) or by rivers that flow through cracks in rock.

GLACIER CAVES
They are formed by melting ice within a glacier.

The longest cave system in the world is Mammoth Cave in Kentucky, 405 mi (651.8 km).

The deepest known cave is Voronya Cave in the country of Georgia, 7,208 ft (2,197 m).

The largest cave in the world is the Sarawak Chamber in Sarawak, Malaysia.

Stalactites

Helictites

Column

Stalagmites

STALACTITES AND STALAGMITES

Stalactites form from the continuous dripping of mineral-rich water from the ceilings of caves. As the minerals slowly settle and harden, icicle-shaped encrustations form on the ceiling.

When the water drops fall to the ground, they leave mineral deposits that grow upwards, forming stalagmites. If they get very big, they look like pillars.

Stalactites and stalagmites can also join together to form columns. However, they grow very slowly, about 1 in (2.5 cm) every 100 years.

A CAVE is an ecosystem that we can divide into FOUR zones:

(1) **ENTRANCE ZONE:** This is the "door" between the outside world and the underground world. It's quite bright, and the temperature is similar to outside the cave.

(2) **TWILIGHT ZONE:** The light gradually decreases. Some plants, such as ferns, mosses, and algae, can grow as far as the sun's rays can reach.

(3) **TRANSITION ZONE:** No light reaches this zone, although other environmental factors, such as temperature and humidity, are still affected by external conditions.

(4) **DARK ZONE:** Here there is perpetual darkness, high humidity, and a low evaporation rate. The temperature remains constant all year round. The animals found in this zone have specific adaptations in order to survive.

CAVES were important in prehistoric times for shelter, for burials, and as religious places.

Many **BATS** take shelter in caves during the day, coming out at night to look for insects and fruit. Their excrement serves as nourishment for detritivorous animals, such as mites and beetles, which in turn are preyed upon by spiders, scorpions, and scolopendras.

FAUNA

Caves are certainly not easy places to live. They are dark, cold, and very humid, and there is little food. Despite this, there is no shortage of animal species, such as bats, foxes, hedgehogs, salamanders, insects, and spiders, which have chosen caves as a safe home to live, either occasionally or permanently.

WHITE TO PINKISH IN COLOR
due to lack of pigmentation because they don't need protection from the sun's rays or to camouflage themselves.

NO EYES OR VERY SMALL EYES
Sight is useless where there's no light.

LONGER LEGS AND ANTENNAS
to move around easier and to feel their surroundings.

Animals that live in caves have adapted to the darkness and often have unique characteristics.

3

The underground waters in karst caves are home to the **OLM**, an amphibian relative of the salamander. It has two red tufts on either side of its head, which are its gills. It keeps these throughout its life (unlike most amphibians which metaphorize into terrestrial forms) as it has adapted to remain aquatic by not metaphorizing.

Colonies made up of millions of BATS can live in some caves.

IS THE EARTH IN DANGER?

As you have seen, Earth is unique and extraordinary.
Yet, the actions of humans risk ruining our planet forever.

GLOBAL WARMING

Carbon dioxide (CO_2) is a gas that naturally occurs in the
atmosphere and helps heat Earth through a process called the
greenhouse effect. However, due to human activities, the amount
of CO_2 and other gases, such as methane, is increasing. This is
causing the planet to heat up at an unusually rapid rate, kind of
like a fever, because our atmosphere
is absorbing more and more heat.

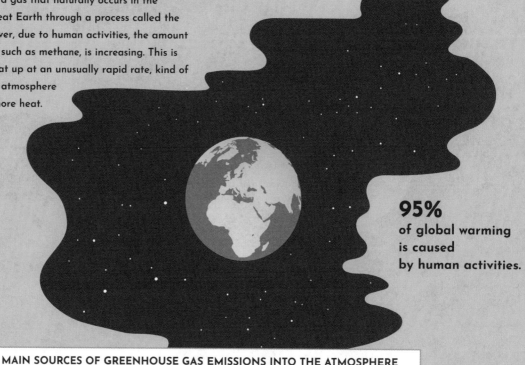

95%
of global warming
is caused
by human activities.

MAIN SOURCES OF GREENHOUSE GAS EMISSIONS INTO THE ATMOSPHERE

**Consumption of
fossil fuels (oil and
coal) to produce
electricity**

**Waste
disposal
systems**

**Agriculture
and intensive
farming**

**Factories
and industries**

**Heating
in houses, offices,
and stores**

**Transportation
(cars, trains,
planes, and
ships)**

This "extra" heat affects not only the temperature, but also the wind,
ocean currents, and all meteorological phenomena. Global warming
is therefore changing the climate in many regions on Earth.

Furthermore, the oceans are absorbing more and more carbon
dioxide from the atmosphere. This reacts with the water and
forms carbonic acid, which makes our oceans more acidic and
severely damages the marine environment.

MELTING GLACIERS

One consequence of global warming is that the glaciers are melting. The polar ice caps and high mountain ranges, such as the Alps, the Andes, and the Himalayas, are progressively losing large amounts of ice that accumulated over hundreds of years.

Glaciers in the Alps have shrunk by **60%** over the past 150 years.

Between 2004 and 2016 (12 years), the Bridge Glacier in Canada retreated almost 2 miles (3 km).

The effect on the polar ice caps is even more evident and dramatic, especially in the Arctic; today, the temperature is 3 degrees higher than it was 150 years ago.

Over the past 40 years, the surface area of the Arctic ice cap has shrunk by 35%. It has lost an area seven times the size of California!

The melting ice and glaciers inevitably cause sea levels to rise. The water needs to rise only a few more feet before coastal cities like Miami or cities built on lagoons, like Venice, Italy, are submerged.

Arctic

-35% of the polar ice cap

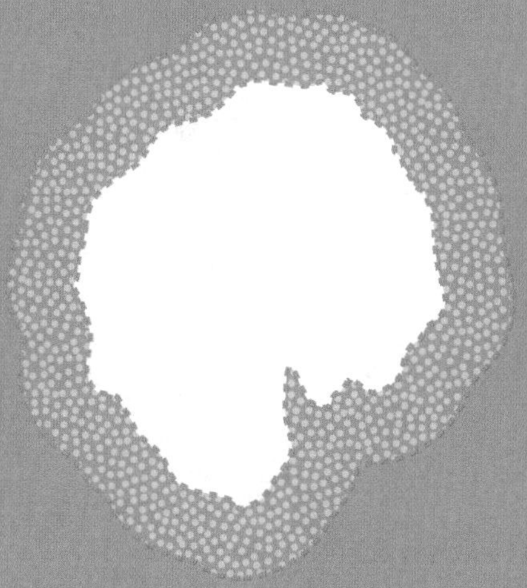

Today, sea levels are rising at a rate of around 3.4 millimeters per year, and it is estimated that they have already risen by 8 in (20 cm) over the last century. By 2100, the levels could rise by 24-35 inches (60-90 cm).

+8 inches (20 cm)

DEFORESTATION

A not-so-green Earth

Forests are disappearing, and the speed at which this is happening is alarming; scientists have calculated that every minute, an area the size of 40 football fields "vanishes" before our eyes!

DEFORESTATION happens in various ways: fires, tree-cutting to make way for fields, cattle grazing, and construction, the overexploitation of trees for timber, and also degradation due to climate change.

Forests are a habitat for numerous animal and plant species, and when their home is taken away from them, they gradually disappear.

Trees are extremely important because they absorb carbon dioxide from the atmosphere, thereby reducing the greenhouse effect. It is estimated that 15% of all greenhouse gas emissions are the result of deforestation.

Also, plants hold the soil with their roots, thereby limiting erosion and reducing the risk of landslides, especially following heavy rain.

DESERTIFICATION
Less and less water

Desertification is a natural phenomenon that causes the planet's arid and semiarid areas to turn into deserts. Global warming, however, is speeding up the process.

CAUSES OF DESERTIFICATION IN TEMPERATE ZONES

Intensive agriculture

Intensive animal farming

Global warming

Recently, desertification has also been occurring in temperate zones. Intensive agriculture and excessive grazing exploit the soil too quickly, not leaving enough time for it to regenerate. Depleted of its nutrients, the soil becomes unproductive.

AN ATTACK ON BIODIVERSITY

A world that changes too quickly puts the living organisms it is home to at risk. Scientists are sounding the alarm; in a few decades, **75%** of Earth's living species could become extinct—that is, disappear forever!

This event would greatly reduce biodiversity, the incredibly rich variety of living beings that populate Earth and depend on each other to survive.

Although **EXTINCTION** is a natural phenomenon that has always occurred on Earth, it is quite clear that humans have significantly accelerated its occurrence.

Today, extinction is more and more a consequence of climate change, pollution, poaching, overfishing, and the destruction of habitats caused by humans and their activities.

DragonFruit, an imprint of Mango Publishing, publishes high-quality children's books to inspire a love of lifelong learning in readers. DragonFruit publishes a variety of titles for kids, including children's picture books, nonfiction series, toddler activity books, pre-K activity books, science and education titles, and ABC books. Beautiful and engaging, our books celebrate diversity, spark curiosity, and capture the imaginations of parents and children alike.

Mango Publishing, established in 2014, publishes an eclectic list of books by diverse authors. We were named the Fastest-Growing Independent Publisher by Publishers Weekly in 2019 and 2020. Our success is bolstered by our main goal, which is to publish high-quality books that will make a positive impact in people's lives.

Our readers are our most important resource; we value your input, suggestions, and ideas. We'd love to hear from you—after all, we are publishing books for you!

Please stay in touch with us and follow us at:
Instagram: @dragonfruitkids
Facebook: Mango Publishing
Twitter: @MangoPublishing
LinkedIn: Mango Publishing
Pinterest: Mango Publishing

Sign up for our newsletter at www.mangopublishinggroup.com and receive a free book! Join us on Mango's journey to change publishing, one book at a time.